JAMES HETFIELD

THE WOLF AT METALLICA'S DOOR

MARK EGLINTON

Published in 2010 by
INDEPENDENT MUSIC PRESS
Independent Music Press is an imprint of I.M. P. Publishing Limited
This Work is Copyright © I. M. P. Publishing Ltd 2010

James Hetfield – The Wolf At Metallica's Door
by Mark Eglinton

British Library Cataloguing-in-Publication Data.
A catalogue for this book is available from The British Library.
ISBN: 978-1-906191-04-7

Cover Design by Fresh Lemon.
Cover photograph courtesy of Paul Bergen/Getty Images.

Printed in Finland.

Independent Music Press
P.O. Box 69,
Church Stretton, Shropshire
SY6 6WZ
Visit us on the web at: www.impbooks.com
and www.myspace.com/independentmusicpress
For a free catalogue, e-mail us at: info@impbooks.com
Fax: 01694 720049

James Hetfield

The Wolf At Metallica's Door

by Mark Eglinton

Independent Music Press

NOTE FROM THE PUBLISHER

It is a sad fact that Metallica's lead singer James Hetfield lost both of his parents to cancer. Given this is an unofficial and unauthorised book, with no official involvement from James Hetfield or Metallica, the publisher – Independent Music Press – will be donating 25 pence from every copy sold to Cancer Research UK, as a gesture of goodwill.

CONTENTS

Foreword

I can't remember the exact year it was when we all first met but I know it was way before Metallica came into their own and became the band that they are today. Having mutual friends, we used to go to a lot of New Year's parties and such. Seeing James perform for the first time I was truly taken aback. It was great watching this guy perform. I went to the party expecting to see James singing and playing guitar but he was playing drums, which blew me away. He was even more cooler than before. James made a huge imprint on the Bay Area with his distinct sound and attitude. He used to perform with the band Spastic Children whose lead singer was Fred Cotton. Back then it really was all about good times and fun. From day one, James was the guy who started the movement and carried it out to the finish. In my mind he is one of the, if not *the* best metal guitarist/lyricist, for sure.

Thinking back, I can remember the moment when I knew that Metallica had really hit it big. I was playing in a basketball league at my local gym, a gym that happened to serve beer by the way... After the game was over they were going to debut the new Metallica video. They dropped down a 50-inch projection screen and we waited. The video started. This was the first time I experienced the Metallica video for 'Enter Sandman'. For the band that never did videos and didn't care about airplay, they surely made one hell of a video! Watching it I said to myself "Holy Smokes..." I knew from then on that Metallica was going to be one of the biggest bands ever.

Another story about James and Metallica that I will never forget took place on a sunny Sunday during our normal tailgate party for the Oakland Raiders. Every Sunday we all used to get together and tailgate before the games. On this particular Sunday, a rumour was going around that Metallica was going to be playing in the parking lot prior to the game. When I heard this I immediately thought it was bullshit, but people seemed to be sure that it was going to happen. Sure enough, on the other side of the parking lot there was a flat-bed truck that was sealed up on all of the sides. Something was going on. When I saw the cars parked by the truck and Hetfield get out, the grin on his face said it all… the next thing we knew the Metallica guys are heading into the flat-bed. Within minutes, the front opened up and there was Metallica playing live at the tailgate of a Raiders game. This experience was totally mind-blowing and it is something that I will never forget.

And that's one of the coolest things about James and Metallica. No matter how massive they have gotten, they still do unique things, like play a tailgating party or countless other special gigs for their fans. Hopefully this book will rekindle certain special memories about one of metal's most charismatic and important individuals.

Chuck Billy (Testament)

Introduction

"James Hetfield is an unsung virtuoso. His guitar and vocal sound, along with his song ideas, have enabled Metallica to go from being classified alongside Motörhead and Venom, to being aligned with Bruce Springsteen and U2." Those are the weighty words of Alex Skolnick – guitarist with thrash metal pioneers Testament, as well as a member of the Trans Siberian Orchestra and his own band. Skolnick is something of a virtuoso himself, as well as being an astute commentator on the wider world of rock music. While Hetfield's early career was characterised by an aggressive thrust of activity that propelled his band from the underground towards a seat at thrash metal's top table in 1986, it would be their later career impact that has turned out to be considerably more telling.

However, if you'd asked me back in 1986 whether I envisaged writing about and assessing the career and life of James Hetfield then I'm sure the answer would have been no. Equally, if you'd suggested that the distinctly guarded guy I'd met after a show at the Edinburgh Playhouse that year would go on to become a genuine rock icon alongside the likes of stars such as Bono or Springsteen, then the response would probably have been much the same.

As it turns out, a lot has changed in the intervening twenty-four years and the result is this, the first definitive biography of James Hetfield, frontman of Metallica, by far the biggest heavy rock band of the modern era.

September 12, 1986: Metallica along with New York thrashers Anthrax were playing on the British leg of their 'Damage Inc.' tour to open-mouthed metal audiences throughout Europe. This tour more than any served to properly introduce UK audiences to thrash metal and this would affect a change in the fabric of heavy music thereafter, with far more emphasis being placed on speed and downright aggression. Not just that, Metallica had by this time in their career also acquired a knack for complex song structures and this combination of intelligence and utter ferocity was proving a killer mix.

This wasn't a normal tour though because Hetfield – not for the last time as it would turn out – had broken bones, on this occasion his left wrist, courtesy of a skate-boarding accident earlier that year while negotiating a hill in Evanston, Indiana. The result was a plaster cast, which inevitably ruled out any guitar antics for many of the dates on that tour.

Fortunately, John Marshall – the guitar technician of Kirk Hammett, Metallica's other guitarist – was willing and able to fill-in on rhythm duties from somewhere in the wings while the band raged on-stage with Hetfield limited to vocal involvement. Later in the tour, and despite initial and understandable reluctance, Marshall was encouraged to actually join the band on-stage which must surely have been a surreal experience given the utter frenzy that greeted these classic shows. Somewhat ironically, Hetfield's now legendary ability as a rhythm guitarist of almost inhuman precision was the one thing we didn't witness first-hand that night, but his barked vocals and intimidating stage presence definitely left a lasting impression.

As if that night wasn't memorable enough, after the show Hetfield and the late Cliff Burton, Metallica's bass player at the time, wandered into a bar down the street from the venue where a few of us were drinking and discussing the gig. Through a haze of time and alcohol, I vaguely recall a brief chat ensuing and certainly remember Burton being by far the more forthcoming of the two, with Hetfield preferring a more distant approach. Not that it mattered to any of us though, as to meet any of the band after such a life-changing show was a huge bonus; from that day I always felt that our paths had crossed on some level, though I'm sure to them it was just an easily forgotten meeting with fans.

It goes without saying that the raw, evolving Metallica of back then was a very different band from the monster they were to become, given that their commercial zenith was still some five years away. Similarly, the personalities involved have undergone considerable development over the years because of the band's huge commercial success and the accompanying public scrutiny that comes with it. From day one though, the driving force behind Metallica has always been the axis of Hetfield and drummer Lars Ulrich, and that relationship over the years has often been strained on a personal level – hardly surprising given their wildly different personal backgrounds. Through it all, particularly pre-1992, the aural results have been impossible to question though, and Hetfield's influential role in that forms a significant part of this work.

Apart from identifying Hetfield as a guitarist of other-worldly ability, a frontman of gargantuan stature and a much-underrated lyricist and song-writer, the book also has another purpose other than merely placing the man in the pantheon of great and influential rock musicians. That is to establish whether James Hetfield is in fact a more sensitive and caring person than the public persona that has been projected over the years. We're well aware of that image of the hirsute, hard-drinking man of hunting and hot-rods, but that's not all he is.

Here we try to understand, de-mystify and even humanize a rock legend that for most of his career has remained impenetrable ... hopefully, if you're not a particular fan of his music you'll enjoy this book on a purely human level. You might even find yourself being sucked into the exhilarating world of Metallica as a result, in which case the seed is sown and my job is done.

It's been nothing short of humbling to receive a level of unconditional and generous support from so many important people – within the context of this book at least – most of whom I have never actually met in the flesh. Without it all, this biography would certainly have been a lesser beast, and possibly may not even have existed at all. Heavy metal truly is a tight-knit community and one where treating people with respect – an old school value perhaps – lives on to this day. Remember, these were the days before the internet and the mobile phone, and info about awesome bands playing in the Bay Area and memorable shows was often relayed back to Los Angeles and other areas via letters between friends with similar interests. Some of these buddies are here in this book as a result – a few of them discussing events for the first time

— and it's been an honour to exist in their world for even a short part of my life.

It was a conversation with Joel McIver back in 2005 I believe, which represented the beginning of this journey. I had just read his excellent *Justice For All: The Truth About Metallica* (if you haven't read it, you need to immediately, but *after* you've finished this of course) and he made the mistake of including his e-mail address ...

Thereafter sporadic communication occurred over the next couple of years, mostly about Metallica but also about more normal matters. Without Joel — and he knows why — I would not be writing this book and I'll always be grateful. Cheers mate, sincerely.

Of the others who have helped there is a list which is in no particular order, and they're *all* important: Martin Roach and Dave Hanley at Independent Music Press, Chuck Billy (Testament) for his Foreword, Ron Quintana, Brian Slagel (Metal Blade), Bill Hale, Brian Lew, Ron McGovney, Mike Tacci, Eric Braverman, Fred Cotton, David Ellefson, Charlie Benante (Anthrax), Bob Nalbandian (Hardradio), Jerry Cantrell (Alice In Chains), Brian Fair (Shadows Fall), Malcolm Dome (Total Rock Radio), Eric Braverman, David Tedder, Katon de Pena (Hirax), John Doran and Luke Turner (The Quietus), Alex Skolnick (Testament, Trans Siberian Orchestra and The Alex Skolnick Trio), Dave Marrs, Hugh Tanner, John Kornarens, Michael Alago, Flemming Rasmussen, Lloyd Grant, Mille Petrozza (Kreator), Lonn Friend, Bobby Schneider, Dan Beehler (Exciter, Beehler), Jeff Waters (Annihilator), Michael Wagener, Sammy DeJohn, Jim Durkin (Dark Angel), Rex Brown (Pantera, Down), Rikki Zazula (Adrenaline PR), James Arnold and Jonny Zazula.

On a personal level, the following people have given me invaluable personal support: Yvonne Modu, Mum, Richard and Michele, Andrew Eglinton, Jack Eglinton, Al Rutherford, Ren Rhodes, Seth Chappell, and my growing list of Facebook friends, without whom this project would have taken at least half the time it did!

Mark Eglinton
Essex, England, 2010

CHAPTER 1

Jamie

It's a matter of continual debate whether the traits human beings carry through life are determined at birth as a result of genetic inheritance, or whether we exhibit them on account of our upbringing and environment. While it is entirely possible that both factors contribute to our finished form, there is little doubt that the early years of a person's life are particularly absorbent of the effects of stress and family upheaval.

As environments go, Downey, California is as neutral and unremarkable as many of the other towns in the area. With a history that dates back to the Spanish colonial times of the early 1770s, the city of today is located at the confluence of several major highways, at a point approximately thirteen miles south-east of the bright lights and perceived opportunity of downtown Los Angeles.

It consists of three distinct areas: South Downey, which is lower income, Mid-Downey, more middle income, and the Northern part of Downey, which is the up-scale part of town. Be in no doubt however: Downey is not on the traditional LA tourist trail, although Disneyland is relatively close in nearby Norwalk.

The oldest surviving McDonalds restaurant is located on Downey's Lakewood Boulevard, having been there since 1953. It really says a lot about the city's heritage that a fast food restaurant should be one of its few protected structures, and to complete the set, Taco Bell opened their first ever restaurant in Downey in 1962. Despite a history steeped in fast food folklore, Downey is really just a working-class suburban town.

Approximately one year after Downey residents inherited that dubious ability to eat tacos in public, James Alan Hetfield was born on August 3, 1963. Put in context, this was a momentous year in musical terms for Downey, not just because a future rock icon was born, but also because singing siblings The Carpenters moved there from their native Connecticut.

James Hetfield's mother Cynthia – a light opera singer – had been previously married prior to meeting James's father Virgil. Cynthia was, as her son James once described her, "a Berkeley Mom", and was apparently reasonably open to loud music and long hair. Virgil on the other hand was a truck driver by trade, with a small distribution operation of his own. Subsequently, Cynthia undertook the bulk of the childcare in the early days, as James's father would often be away from home on extended business trips, and although widely known to be a kind man, he was – in contrast to his more laid-back wife – considerably more reserved and conservative.

James had two half brothers, Chris and Dave, who were eleven and twelve years older, as well as a sister Deandra. It was a loving environment, and one that encouraged creativity. However, there was one feature that bound them all together ... the Hetfields were a family of faith, and that faith was in the branch of religion known as *The Church of Christian Science*. It is important to be aware of at least the basic parameters of the religion in order to better understand Hetfield and his approach to life as an adult. Although only present in his formative years, this faith influenced some of his life's most important moments, and as such, its influence cannot be flippantly dismissed.

Often confused with the *Church of Scientology*, the two are in fact worlds apart. Christian Science is related to, and shares aspects of what would normally be considered 'regular' (for want of a better word) Christianity. The ultimate focus of worship and belief is God. Founded in 1866 by Mary Baker Eddy from New Hampshire – a woman who had endured considerable chronic childhood illness – the belief system maintains, among other things, that the power of healing is available to all of us, and that we need simply refer to Biblical scriptures for all the answers. The church also considers the universe and all humanity to be of a spiritual nature as opposed to being material entities. Confused? Hold on, there is more to it than just that ...

The suggestion is also that due to the 'absolute purity' and perfection of God, sin, disease and death could not have been created by him, so therefore they do not exist. Importantly for the purposes of this discussion though, it is considered that a spiritual healing system is by far preferable to conventional medicine when it comes to dealing with illness and disease. Healing through prayer is a central tenet of their belief system (medicine is not forbidden, but prayer is the preferred route for many). It is this limitation that would become particularly pertinent for the Hetfield family in future years, and it is a feature of his upbringing that James expressed some discomfort towards in later life.

In fact, he spelled it out pretty clearly to *Playboy* magazine when reflecting on his childhood in an interview in 2001. "I was raised a Christian Scientist, which is a strange religion. The main rule is: God will fix everything. Your body is just a shell, you don't need doctors. It was alienating and hard to understand." This unusual outlook and very restrictive approach to medicine would impact significantly on both the Hetfield family and James himself as his adolescent life progressed.

When asked if he ever resisted the guidelines his family laid down, Hetfield explained in the same *Playboy* interview: "Once, me and my sister split. Our parents caught us about four blocks away. They spanked the shit out of us, pretty much."

James was close to his half-brothers, and David in particular was a big influence being several years older (Chris was naturally less prominent having left the family home already). Even at a very early age, young James was steered in a musical direction, mainly by his mother who encouraged him down that familiar route of piano lessons. Starting at the age of nine, these continued for almost two years and he showed a lot of promise, but by his own admission, it wasn't entirely a fulfilling experience playing just classical tunes. That was understandable given that it wasn't the music that kids in California were hearing on the radio at the time and that factor alone made the piano a predictably short-lived distraction.

It wasn't entirely wasted time though, and in recent year James has even acknowledged the importance of that early exposure to a two-handed instrument, even if the results back then weren't exactly what he was looking for. He also admitted rather sheepishly that the cookies that were offered, presumably as an incentive at the end of each session, were a big draw too.

Before long Hetfield's young head was being turned by his older half-brother David's drum kit, and the louder and rockier options it might offer. By that time David was already in a band of his own, and was regularly playing drums in an outfit called The Bitter End, and it was a matter of 'when' rather than 'if' his younger sibling was to head in the same direction armed with a new and burning desire to play the guitar.

Like most young kids, James had his favourite bands and a lot of these were some of the heavier acts of the time, like Black Sabbath, ZZ Top and KISS. However if there was one band which above all others fuelled the desire to rock-out, it was Aerosmith.

Aerosmith at that time were a blues-influenced, swaggering rock band with a heavy lineage derived from the likes of the Rolling Stones. It's common knowledge that they liked to party, and from all reports were a pretty debauched outfit during the 1970s. However, despite living on the edge somewhat, they somehow still managed to prop themselves up on-stage long enough to do live shows in the area which James would one day attend (a 1978 LA Forum show would be the first).

In Joe Perry, Aerosmith had an ice-cool guitarist that definitely caught James's eye and that kind of image was definitely a role he could see himself mirroring. The other bands were influences too but in Perry, James had an object for his ambition more than any other artist at that time.

He was fortunate too that David was at college – training to be a public accountant – which meant that he was often away from home studying. Consequently his considerable record collection – which included not only hard rock bands but a load of old rock 'n' roll 45s – was at the mercy of young James who took full advantage and used his brother's vinyl horde and made it his bedrock of influence.

It didn't go un-noticed by David however, and as part of a documentary some years later called *Some Kind Of Monster*, James sheepishly admitted: "I'd always leave the turntable on and he'd know. I'd come home and get busted because the turntable was still on." David seemed to always know what his younger brother was up to, as Hetfield himself admitted when describing getting found out: "'Jamie, were you playing my records?' He called me Jamie when I was a kid."

Another guy around the Downey scene in those days was Ron McGovney, a character whose very existence plays a major and often under-valued role in the band we now know as Metallica. McGovney definitely felt that he and James were kindred spirits back in those days. Ron remembers how they got together: "We met at East Middle School in Downey at the age of about eleven. We both went to different elementary schools, so we didn't know each other before then. I really lived in Norwalk, the next city over, but my parents got me into Downey schools, which they thought were better."

In McGovney, James clearly had a like-minded friend but at that stage you wouldn't say that their musical tastes were particularly well aligned, although that would gradually change as Ron explained: "Neither of us was in any social or sports group. We were the outcasts, you might say. He used to make fun of my Elvis sticker I had on my folder, and I made fun of the Aerosmith sticker he had on his." As far as his own 'conversion' to hard music goes, Ron went on, "He is the one who really got me into listening to hard rock and metal. Before that, I listened to stuff like the Doobie Brothers, Fleetwood Mac and, of course, Elvis Presley."

It's worth noting McGovney's mention of sport, because due to his family's religious beliefs, James did not always participate in the kind of active physical involvement in sports for fear of getting badly hurt. It makes sense therefore that the absence of the kind of bonding experience that young children find in team sports must have been a significant reason for his apparent quiet demeanour, with only his growing interest in music to rely on.

In addition to being marginalised from team sports – an activity that is generally considered to be part and parcel of most teenagers' lives – Hetfield was clearly starting to ask some questions about his family's religious beliefs. As part that retrospective discussion with *Playboy* magazine in 2001, Hetfield suggested that he clearly found the health implications of his religious upbringing difficult to understand: "My dad taught Sunday school – he was into it. It was pretty much forced upon me. We had these little testimonials, and there was a girl that had her arm broken. She stood up and said, 'I broke my arm but now, look, it's all better.' But it was just, like, mangled. Now that I think about it, it was pretty disturbing."

Despite some of the more challenging aspects of his religious exposure, James was starting to find his feet and recognising that music was something he really did enjoy. Unfortunately, there was a life-changing roadblock looming large, and it came in the form of his parent's divorce in 1976 – an event that understandably shook the family unit to the core.

Hetfield explained to *Playboy* the manner by which he came to know about it: "Dad went on a 'business trip' ... for more than a few years, you know? I was beginning junior high. It was hidden that he was gone. Finally, my Mom said, 'Dad is not coming back'. And that was pretty difficult."

Daily life was perhaps understandably more tense in the household at times, and while Cynthia worked hard to balance home and a career – with inevitable pressure to be at home – James and his sister squabbled frequently, as siblings do. This even escalated to one occasion when James burnt his sister with hot oil, an event that he would later admit was a step or two too far.

Perhaps the absence of a male father figure at home probably did not help. What wasn't immediately apparent at that juncture however was that Cynthia was also suffering from cancer which, given her religious beliefs, was not going to be an easy battle.

As if there weren't enough challenges for the family at the time, money, or rather lack of it, also became a pressing issue. Consequently, James soon found himself in the position of having to bring in some income for the household by getting a job.

As an aspiring rock star in his own mind, regular work wasn't something he was particularly keen on, and to make matters worse, his mother insisted that nobody would even think about hiring him unless he cut his hair. This, according to James, wasn't happening anytime soon. "Well, long hair's part of music, Mom. Y'know, if I've got short hair I can't rock, you know. There's no way," Hetfield later recalled saying.

Long hair still intact, music continued to be the chosen escape and at this stage James was actively seeking to join or ideally form his own band. As well as Ron McGovney, another fellow pupil called Dave Marrs had a similar taste for late 1970s rock (initially unbeknown to each other). As a result, it was perhaps inevitable for them to gravitate together.

"Ron and I were actually friends first, and we all knew James but he was never into our little clique of friends that we had," Dave told the author. "Then in tenth grade I had him in a biology class and I had my KISS t-shirt on and he had his Aerosmith shirt on and we just became really good friends. Everything kind of clicked from there."

So James, Ron and Dave were running in the same circles – largely based on their love of music – and this was a bond that would last for several years to come. The group would spend time doing the kinds of things kids do, which in Downey meant hanging around the local miniature golf course where there were video games, or the local bowling alley where the trio spent free time playing on the pool tables. Nothing out of the ordinary, just regular teenage life in suburban California.

School days continued in late 1970s Downey with rock music taking a position high up the pecking order for this group of like-minded teenagers. While James spent most of his time thinking about how to get in some kind of band, he wasn't totally without talent in other departments. "I would say he was a pretty [normal] student generally," McGovney remembers. "Practising guitar took up a lot of his time! Even then it was obvious that music was the way forward. But he did excel at art classes though and could probably have made a career out of that", McGovney adds.

That early artistic talent is something that would prove useful in future years, and Hetfield's ability to create an image – whether it be artistically for an album cover, or lyrically for a song – would be of intrinsic value to his future role in all his bands, most notably Metallica.

As much as James wanted to form a band and as desperately as he aspired to be the driving force behind it, the outfit that would offer James his first chance to rock – called simply Obsession – was really the brainchild of a couple of brothers called Ron and Rich Veloz. Marrs tells the story succinctly: "I was real good friends with the Veloz brothers and they had something going on with their band. They had another friend with them called Jim Arnold as well. They said, 'We need another guitar player', and that's how James ended up joining Obsession."

Arnold himself told the author about the first time he went round to James's house: "The thing I remember most is that he had a life-sized silhouette on his bedroom wall. From what I remember, it was Steve Tyler and Joe Perry of Aerosmith, and I think he said his mother had painted it for him. It was very cool!"

Obsession would consist of Hetfield on guitar, two brothers Ron and Rich Veloz on bass and drums, and Jim Arnold on lead guitar. Any band needs a kick-ass road crew so McGovney and Marrs were drafted in as exactly that, although Marrs admitted that their role was maybe a little overstated: "We were more like friends than actually roadies really."

The Veloz boys had a garage and that space became the venue for rehearsals with Marrs and McGovney staffing some kind of crude control panel to give the place some basic lighting effects. Marrs remembers the details: "They just played like back-yard parties back then. They were just like your average garage band. They did UFO covers, and I think they did 'Communication Breakdown', good songs like that. I remember that the Veloz brothers [had] some traffic lights or something, and they hooked them up into the garage and we'd go up there and play with the lights. We were fifteen-year-old kids and we didn't know what we were actually doing up there, we definitely didn't. It was a good time back then though."

Jim Arnold lived down the street at the time, and he too has fond memories of Obsession's early garage days: "We built a wall inside that garage and soundproofed one half of it using old cardboard and carpet. James only lived a few miles from there and he would use his mom's car to drive over, or we would go and pick him up. We spent a lot of time in that garage; it was our party and practice place."

Although no actual recordings of the band in action exist, it is fairly safe to say that the Hetfield of Obsession days and the one we all know now are poles apart. His voice at the time had little of the full-bore bellow that he would develop in the late 1980s and definitely none of the honest harmony that would almost apologetically bleed into their work in the commercial heyday of the 1990s. His guitar playing too – literally a *Terminator*-like act of unstoppable brutality in later years – was reputedly only just about passable in those formative Obsession days. He was, after all, still only a teenager.

Far from being a diet consisting solely of hard rock, Hetfield's musical tastes were pretty diverse as an adolescent and like most teenagers discovering the buzz of concert-going, the group of friends would pretty much take in any gig they could in the area – relying on lifts from patient parents to venues in the wider LA sprawl.

Marrs recalls one of them in particular: "I actually remember going to a Blondie concert with James back then. It was in the Greek Theatre, which is in LA, and I can remember his mom taking us there and then my mom came to pick us up. It was just weird to see Blondie and stuff with James and now you have to consider that they're both in the Rock 'n' Roll Hall Of Fame."

So, with a lack of variety that goes with the territory of a band playing mainly generic covers, Obsession's days were very much numbered from the start. The fact that none of them could decide who would sing probably didn't help much either and so James traded vocal duties with Jim Arnold and Ron Veloz, depending on which cover version they happened to be doing.

After only about eighteen months however, James and Jim Arnold left Obsession to form a new project with Jim's brother Chris, entitled simply Syrinx, and that band would play covers of influential Canadian prog-rock three piece Rush.

The origin of the name was presumably pretty obvious: 'Temple Of Syrinx' from Rush's seminal concept record *2112*. This band was also to be another short-lived arrangement. Luckily, there was a more durable band project just around the corner whose existence would have a telling effect on the direction of James's career. "James was very cool and fun to be around," Jim Arnold confirms, "but more importantly, he introduced us to a lot of cool music that was not mainstream at the time: Scorpions, Rush, Iron Maiden and bands like that. Back then we had never heard of such bands."

Lurking in the background however was a far bigger issue, and one that would have huge impact on the Hetfield family unit. For a long while – and amid rapidly failing health – James's mother Cynthia found it easier to hide her illness away from the kids. Before too long she had become sufficiently ill to need hospital attention, but she declined conventional medical treatment.

Cynthia passed away in 1979, leaving the kids in an understandably extremely confused emotional place. After the sad passing of his mother – while James was in the eleventh grade – he moved to nearby Brea to live with half-brother David who had recently got married. Although he rarely discussed the constraints of his religious upbringing, there is little doubt that such huge upheaval crammed into only a few years must have taken an emotional toll. Perhaps a sensation of a lack of control over his personal circumstances was inevitable, and this would become a key part of Hetfield's life from here on, manifesting itself in numerous forms.

Dave Marrs remembers how that sad news came as a complete shock: "We were outside between classes and James said, 'Well, I'm going to have to move to Brea,' and we said, 'Why are you going to do that?' and James told us, 'My mom just passed away.' We never knew she was sick, we never knew anything. You have to remember, I was always with him and his mother – spending nights at his house and stuff like that – so it was pretty hard. He moved to live with his stepbrother. I kept in real good contact with him, even though he was living further away. As a matter of fact we used to go over there quite a bit."

Jim Arnold also kept in touch with James during his time in Brea: "We would talk on the phone, and he'd stay at my parents' house at the weekends. I knew he was breaking off to form a new band and writing music."

While Jim continued to be a friend, he wasn't convinced that James's embryonic career was actually going anywhere. "He would tell me of songs he was writing and that he was going to form a 'Heavy Metal' band. Back then, Heavy Metal was not very popular. At the time I didn't think he would go anywhere with it, but boy was I wrong!"

Living with David in Brea – some fifteen miles east of Downey

– meant that James would attend Brea Olinda High School. Brea is another one of those quiet suburban towns in California, with a population of only 35,000. It is certainly a step up the ladder from the much bigger and grittier Downey, and for a short period, this would be James Hetfield's neighbourhood.

While arriving at a completely new school was undoubtedly an unsettling time for James, particularly given the tragic loss of his mother Cynthia, musically it turned out to be a good move. Before long, a young kid called Jim Mulligan appeared on the scene, a drummer on a mission, it seemed.

The pair had a lot in common and shared the same passion for music in general, although it is worth mentioning that Jim's tastes at that time were considerably more academic than young Hetfield's. Regardless of any stylistic disagreement, the two young friends were soon thrashing out songs during lunch break, creating the kind of noise that sent other kids into hiding. All except for a guy called Hugh Tanner, who totally 'got' what the two were all about.

At that time, punk rock was flavour of the day at Brea Olinda High School. Long hair was not. Tanner was a junior at Brea Olinda High whereas Hetfield was a senior, but the two had some things in common: they were both starting at a new school, they both had long hair, and they both ended up in Mrs Gahn's English class together.

Interestingly, Tanner has never previously discussed his relationship with Hetfield or indeed any other part of his involvement with the band that would become Metallica ... until now: "My involvement with James Hetfield and Lars Ulrich and Metallica has been something speculated on for some time but is something I have shared only with close family. It was not until the internet brought forth 1980s interviews from Ron McGovney and [Metallica's first guitarist, prior to his departure in 1983 to form his own successful band, Megadeth] Dave Mustaine that a few people began to ask me if I was *that* Hugh Tanner. To some I would say yes and to others I would say no."

This time Tanner said 'yes' for the first time in thirty years and agreed to interview for this book; he remembers both the stories and associated events as if it was yesterday. "The [local people]

I was jamming with liked my playing but did not like that I showed up to this jam session with an ugly Gibson ES335! It was much like Ted Nugent's Birdland guitar but had a cutaway at the top. For whatever reason, I could wail on that guitar but it looked like I was a set musician for Billy Ray Cyrus. Fortunately, I did have a knock-off Flying V at home. I was not keen on it because it was maroon. I took the pieces to the school wood-shop to sand it down and refinish it. James ended helping me to refinish the guitar in gloss white which we did in my garage. We got overspray all over my dad's new Mercedes though."

Hetfield and Tanner quickly formed a very close bond and it was obvious that the two would become lasting friends. Tanner was also well aware of the difficult family circumstances under which James had arrived at the school and he maturely recognised the potential problems: "Starting a new school is pretty intimidating to begin with but when you don't really fit in ... things can be tough."

However, despite all the upheaval at school, and the obvious distress caused by the loss of a parent, Hetfield dealt with it all extremely well as Tanner recalls: "Interestingly, James was grounded, likeable, funny and very polite to my parents. He did not talk much about his family loss and all I really knew was that he was living with his step-brother and wife."

Hugh's mother recognised that things might be hard for James, and at one point, she even aired the possibility of James and his sister coming to live with them for a while. She just felt that it might take some pressure off David who was still settling into this own married life. As it turned out though, that thoughtful suggestion was never actually made to James and things remained as they were during his time in Brea.

With a shared interest in heavier music, Hetfield and Tanner pretty much cruised through academic classes, with vastly more attention focused on drawing pictures of stage sets and writing song titles than on the subjects actually being taught. Tanner remembers English classes being particularly 'productive'.

"We spent time drawing pictures of Iron Maiden's 'Eddie' as well as thinking about lyrics and songs," Tanner recalls. What perhaps seemed insignificant back then, was that among such humble and innocent teenage surroundings, Hetfield was already creating the foundations of some tracks that would later appear on Metallica's full debut in 1983 entitled *Kill 'Em All*. Seminal songs that would one day be well-known, like 'Metal Militia', 'Seek And Destroy' and 'Motorbreath' were conceived here by Hetfield, while his good friend Hugh Tanner provided enthusiastic support.

The American bands that were around at the time were no longer hitting the spot for Hetfield and Tanner, as Aerosmith were not heavy enough and KISS were 'bubblegum'. Consequently their heads were turned towards the speed-influenced bands coming out of the UK like Judas Priest, Motörhead and Iron Maiden, as Tanner recalls: "Van Halen's 'Life is a party' attitude was fun, but it did not completely satisfy the pent up adrenaline of a high school boy who didn't know why, but just wanted to break something ..."

Outside of school hours, the pair would continue to bond, which usually involved James going over to the Tanner house to practice. Tanner vividly recalls, "James would come over and we would spend time trading riffs, playing solos and experimenting with turning riffs into actual songs." When teaming up with Marrs and McGovney, James and Hugh would also dip their young toes into the flamboyant 1980 LA music scene, which at that time was populated by a myriad of glam/hair metal bands. Of those, Ratt, Snow and Du Brow (who became Quiet Riot) were some of the better known, and there would be regular shows at the legendary Whisky on Sunset Strip and other places like The Troubadour on Santa Monica Boulevard.

It was the beginning of exciting times in LA with legendary acts like Mötley Crüe waiting in the wings; the group of young friends were wide-eyed at what opportunities were out there as Tanner recalls: "We all used to go up to LA to see the up-and-comers on the club circuit. The four of us had a blast!"

It was an important time in and out of the classroom at Olinda High, and the school confines were of visibly key relevance for being the lyrical origin of some seminal early Metallica songs. Hugh Tanner's own bedroom was similarly important as an unlikely point of conception for the ideology of some of James's early music that underpinned these tracks, as Tanner confirms: "My old room was the birthplace of riff inspirations for these songs. Not just that, there were others which may have been lost or got morphed into other ideas."

Whatever happened, there is little doubt that this key period of Hetfield's teenage life is of huge significance as far as mapping out the direction he and his future bands would ultimately go in. Although the quality of the recorded material was by Tanner's own admission "very, very poor", given that it was mostly documented on an old Teac reel-to-reel his father had brought back from his days as a spy-pilot in Vietnam, it was nonetheless documented at the time and represents a fascinating ground-zero for some of the most important tracks in metal history.

Tanner also remembers Hetfield having a great sense of humour back then too, even though they were both earnestly trying to carve out future rock anthems. "I was experimenting with my first whammy bar and one time it made a noise like a walrus farting. James came to a dead stop and said, 'What the hell was that?' We laughed hysterically." It seems that James in those days had a lot of solid qualities that would make his stoic determination to be a rock star much more likely. Tanner sums him up best: "Guard down ... funny ... laid back but serious ... cool but never lazy ... focused but not overly intense."

It's amusing to note that despite all these worthy attributes, Hetfield was not particularly scholarly or indeed very technical in a musical sense at this early stage, which is something of a surprise given the amazingly disciplined technician he would later become. Tanner did recognise a rare quality in his friend back then though, and it would be one that James would be putting into practice soon with remarkable effect. "What I viewed as his greatest gift," suggests Tanner, "was tying riffs together into a sensible kick-ass song."

This informal jamming group soon became the first real band assembled by James Hetfield entitled Phantom Lord – a name with obvious significance for any fan of Metallica. Phantom Lord was to be a transient affair however with Jim Mulligan on drums, Tanner on guitar and Hetfield on guitar and vocals. Dave Marrs has a good recollection of what Phantom Lord were all about in those days. "They would do just covers of different things like Iron

Maiden etc. They had a song called 'Handsome Ransom' back then and [Hetfield created] a riff similar to the one from 'No Remorse'. Mulligan was a really good drummer, mind you."

Mulligan might have actually been too musically cerebral in outlook for a full-bore rock band. He wasn't into the aggressive, heavy nature of Tanner and Hetfield's material and this was something that both Tanner and Hetfield noticed. "Jim was a great guy, solid drummer and did not rock the boat, but I did not sense the right chemistry." Tanner expands further, "Jim and I had jammed with Scott Bell from the band Joker, and we nailed side one of Rush's *2112*, but Jim was just too intellectual for metal. It didn't fit and James knew it too."

There wasn't really a fixed bass player in that era although several players apart from Scott Bell came in and out, although it really didn't matter because this embryonic outfit's life span would only last a few months, after which James would move back to Downey when graduating from high school in Brea. Hetfield didn't leave Brea without a parting shot though. Touchingly, he sent his school friend a note when he left Brea Olinda High, and his sentiment was that while he wasn't thrilled with some aspects of school life, he had enjoyed playing music. Additionally, Hetfield also suggested that one day they might be in a stadium crushing rock band.

In the portion of the year-book where seniors described their memories of school and plans for the future, Hetfield wrote:

Likes: *heavy metal rock, water skiing, going to concerts.*
Dislikes: *disco, punk.*
Quotes: "*Long Live Rock*".
Plans: *Play music, get rich.*

The move back to Downey coincided with a slice of good fortune too. Ron McGovney's parents had three properties in the area that had been earmarked by the government to be torn down to make way for a major road that would later become the 105 Freeway. As a result, they were very happy to let their son and James live in one of them rent-free until such a time as the houses were flattened. Even better news was that there was also a garage space that was just begging to be turned into a rehearsal studio.

While neither of the two friends were that skilled in DIY, between them they turned the garage into a custom-made band area as McGovney remembers: "We fixed the garage up into a kind of studio and James and I insulated, painted it and put down a red carpet!"

After taking up residence at the McGovney house, it remains unclear exactly when Phantom Lord ceased to be. What seems likely is that the edges of both Phantom Lord and the next band (which would be called Leather Charm) are more than a little blurred, as McGovney himself suggests: "I am quite confused about how things went down. I remember Phantom Lord was really just Hugh and James. Then Leather Charm got together. However I have my high school year book signed by James saying that he 'hopes the Charm will happen'. So maybe Phantom Lord was actually still when we were in high school."

Regardless of the exact timing, Phantom Lord would soon morph into the more glam-sounding Leather Charm – the last stop on the train line that was to become Metallica, and a stop where people would be disembarking too.

One thing that is certain though is that the living arrangement at Ron's house was highly significant in that it allowed James to focus on music in a custom-made space, without having to worry about working a 'real' job to pay rent – quite a luxury for a teenager. It was a pretty settled period and James's father even visited the house occasionally too as McGovney recalls: "I met his father Virgil when he came over to my house that James shared with me. He was very nice to me. He actually knew my parents through the trucking business that they were all involved with."

Leather Charm, the next Hetfield band incarnation – despite still being effectively a rudimentary covers band – was a significant step forward from Phantom Lord and certainly from the youthful Obsession. The main reason was that this band had at least begun properly working on a few more original tunes; interestingly, some of what Hetfield was writing at this point contained elements of what would become 'Hit The Lights.' This well-known track would later appear in finished form on Metallica's debut album *Kill 'Em All* in 1983.

In addition, Hetfield seemed to be harbouring a new need to be seen as more of a commanding frontman, and at this point more than any previously, he genuinely seemed to be seizing control of his musical destiny. Not just that, he was encouraging his buddy McGovney along for the ride, having helped his friend and housemate to take up the bass guitar.

That said, it's still highly likely that the noise that came out of that insulated garage at the McGovney house was much more akin to adolescent ideas than that of a polished rock band. McGovney, who was apparently improving under Hetfield's tuition, still described the output back then as "some really terrible stuff". Among the products was an original composition embarrassingly called 'Hades Ladies', a title so clichéd it thankfully never resurfaced. At least if it did, it was wisely called something else.

Tanner recalls that his own involvement in bands was starting to come under considerable parental pressure too, so much so that he could only continue if the grades at school were okay. "They weren't!" Tanner admitted, and by this time, he was at a crossroads that would define his entire life course.

What he chose was to back-out of a career playing music in a band – which allowed James to take-on full leadership – and although Tanner doesn't completely disappear from the story, his direct musical involvement with Hetfield effectively ends here. "I still cannot explain the tug I had calling me to step aside, versus throwing up a thunderous middle finger and pushing forward," he ponders. "But the ship sailed and I chose to stay on land."

Things were about to change though because across the city in Newport beach, a gawky Danish kid with a taste for the so-called 'New Wave of British Heavy Metal' – or NWOBHM in abbreviated form – was planning his own future, and the crossing of paths which would follow was to conclusively alter the life and career of both him and James Hetfield.

CHAPTER 2

Enter Lars ...

If you had to compare the relative upbringing of James Hetfield and Lars Ulrich you could simply say that they were worlds apart both geographically and in terms of privilege. Without going into minute details of Ulrich's rather liberal family life – which have been well-documented elsewhere – it's important to have a broad understanding at least, in order to grasp how and why the Hetfield and Ulrich axis worked so effectively.

Lars Ulrich was also born in the summer of 1963, but in contrast to working-class Downey, he landed in the affluent northern suburb of Copenhagen called Gentofte. Ulrich's father Torben was an internationally renowned tennis player who travelled the world with his career, but while at home, he also immersed himself in philosophy and film-making, as well as being an accomplished jazz musician.

On a musical level the Ulrich family were rather well connected too, and prior to Lars being born, Torben would travel frequently to London to perform with jazz greats like Humphrey Lyttleton. Consequently, Lars' childhood involved the kind of exposure to music that very few could hope to enjoy and as a result he became obsessed with rock music, with Deep Purple being a particular early favourite.

Even as a fourteen-year-old, Lars already had a drum kit and would spend his time hammering out versions of Deep Purple and KISS songs in his bedroom, while his parents – themselves very musically open-minded – took their son's obvious passion for heavy rock completely in their stride. Ulrich's somewhat privileged upbringing in contrast to the more gritty and working-class childhood experienced by Hetfield would be a critical factor in their future relationship, creating a great chemistry.

In 1980, with Torben's tennis career easing into what you might call the veteran phase, the family made the decision to uproot en-masse and emigrate to California and the wealthy LA suburb of Newport Beach. That town was the obvious choice given that a good friend of Torben's, Australian tennis star Roy Emmerson, already lived there; in fact Lars had already met Emmerson's son Anthony on a trip to Australia when he was a toddler.

There were a few reasons for the move generally but one was that Lars had a fair amount of potential as a young tennis player himself, so the States represented the best training opportunity, not to mention an infinitely more favourable climate than cold Denmark. Not only that, his parents also recognised their son's great passion for music so they certainly felt that a move abroad, even for a short period, would allow Lars's definitive passion to come to the surface. So in August 1980, the Ulrich family left for California.

While tennis remained popular in the supportive environment of Newport Beach, music, specifically heavy music from Europe, was steadily winning the heart and mind of the young Ulrich. Always inquisitive and happily attending Corona del Mar High School, he soon managed to get hold of the now defunct UK magazine *Sounds*, which acted as his direct line into Europe and the NWOBHM, which was gathering steam back in the UK. Ironically, it was the Emmerson family who received the imported magazine, and Lars just had to go over and pick it up, which he did with increasing enthusiasm.

There were very few people tuned into this new British movement at that time. These were the days long before the internet, or file sharing or indeed any means of hearing new bands other than reading about them and sending away for imported singles or tapes. Lars was several steps ahead of the pack even then.

One guy who did know all about the NWOBHM scene, however, was John Kornarens. Three years older than Lars and James, Kornarens grew up in southern California and moved around a bit while he was young, and then in the early 1970s found himself being attracted to heavy music. "As an eight-year-old I was into heavy music," he told the author. "I sent away for my first *K-Tel* record and it had 'You Really Got Me' by The Kinks on it and I just kept coming back to that song." Kornarens also found himself drawn towards Black Sabbath, Led Zeppelin and, as a result of his interest in World War II, he got into Blue Oyster Cult because he liked the military symbol on their *Secret Treaties* album. "I was the only kid in junior high with a BOC t-shirt and I think everyone thought I was some kind of satanic weirdo!"

By the time 1980 rolled around, Kornarens was a huge devotee of heavy rock music; a year earlier, he too had occasionally managed to get his hands on *Sounds* magazine and was attracted to the stuff that nobody else was listening to. "I always tried to be the first guy out of the gate as far as what was new, and was always looking for stuff that was off the radar," John continues. "Through *Sounds* I got into the imported material and sometime in 1980 I got the Angel Witch single."

Angel Witch, while never enjoying the success that bands like Saxon and Iron Maiden achieved, were nevertheless one of the important early exponents of the genre, so to have an imported single of theirs was without doubt something of a coup at that time.

Given the huge population of southern California, it would seem unlikely that the few people that were following a new and distant music scene would be thrown together, particularly as Ulrich lived some sixty miles down the coast. However, get together they did and Kornarens vividly remembers where. "I went to see the Michael Schenker Group at The Country Club, and afterwards in the parking lot I looked and saw a little guy with long hair wearing a Saxon tour shirt. I thought I was the only person in the country who knew who Saxon were!"

The two teenagers were drawn together immediately. "I walked right up to him and we started talking about Saxon. Then I told him I had the new Angel Witch single and he did a back-flip." The two talked for a while about all the bands they liked and as Kornarens remembers, "We made an instant connection."

What happened next is a good example of what makes Lars Ulrich unique. Instead of letting his new friend settle, and maybe re-connecting after a few days or weeks, Ulrich appeared at Kornarens's front door the very next morning – eager to rifle through his record collection. His enthusiasm and passion took the rather laid-back Kornarens by surprise: "He used to drive his mother's car – an old brown AMC Pacer – which was probably the ugliest car ever designed. He came up the next day and we spent hours talking and listening to music."

With clearly a lot in common, Ulrich and Kornarens became good friends quickly as John confirms: "I think I was down at his place a few days later and we kind of became the NWOBHM Beavis and Buttheads!" Having plundered each other's collection, Ulrich and Kornarens would trawl around the record shops of the LA area to look for new material. "We'd drive up to places like Moby Disc and see what new stuff they had," Kornarens remembers.

Prior to meeting Ulrich, Kornarens had picked up an interesting fanzine entitled *The New Heavy Metal Review*, and that fanzine was founded by a tape-trader called Brian Slagel from Woodland Hills – an area out west of LA.

At the time, buying traded tapes was one of the only ways of hearing about new bands, and as a result a network of tape-traders quickly sprang up, and their primary business was to mail tapes of bands and demos to like-minded fans, some of them overseas. It was the equivalent of internet file-sharing as we have today except the quality at that time was sometimes very poor, given that the recordings were often third-hand or more.

Regardless of the rough quality, traded tapes were a massive part of the music scene and Brian Slagel was one of the first in the LA area to get seriously into it. "He was just into trading stuff and I first got a hold of him [when] I went out to his house to collect some heavy stuff I'd ordered," Kornarens remembers.

However, as Ulrich and Kornarens saw more of each other, Brian Slagel was gradually absorbed into the group, and that connection was one that would prove of vital importance to the joint destiny of Ulrich and Hetfield in the near future. In the meantime, Kornarens, Ulrich and Slagel would tour the area looking for new material that nobody had. "We'd go record shopping in my old Volkswagen Scirocco and I was always the point guy," John recalls.

Given that most of these record shops were scattered around

way-out places like Long Beach or Torrance, it usually meant that Kornarens had to drive and pick the other two up. "Brian would be in the front and Lars would be in the back and when we arrived at each record store, Lars would somehow manage to climb over Brian to get out, even when the car hadn't come to a complete stop!"

Ulrich was always keen to get the first look at the record bins. "By the time we got there, Lars had probably been through three racks, and found the only copy of this band or that band!" Kornarens concedes. As well as patrolling the neighbourhood with Slagel like some kind of unstoppable record buying delta-force, Kornarens and Ulrich also ordered new material from adverts they saw in *Sounds* magazine and Lars would stop at nothing to get what he wanted. "We'd ordered the new Holocaust record or something and Lars called one day to say the package had arrived."

What Kornarens did not know before his hour-long drive to Newport Beach was that there was, as Lars put it, "a problem with John's Holocaust record". What had actually happened is that Ulrich had opened the package and put one of the records on the stove – where it got badly warped – and this unsurprisingly was Kornarens's copy. "And the next day I even tried to get my mother to iron the fucking thing out!" Kornarens laughs.

As 1980 moved into 1981, the distance between Ulrich and Hetfield was shrinking, given the tight-knit nature of the LA metal scene. Not just that, unknown to each of them, they had a common link from earlier in the story in the form of Hugh Tanner. "I came across Lars when James and I were still jamming together because I answered an ad in the *Recycler* magazine where Lars listed himself as a 'drummer from Europe'." Tanner remembers. Ulrich's advert also mentioned a whole raft of NWOBHM bands.

"So I called and we jammed," Tanner confirms. Also at that first session was guitarist Jeff 'Woop' Warner, who according to Tanner had a good rock 'n' roll look and sound. Warner would later join hair metal band Black N Blue but that first session made Tanner think that Hetfield's need to be a frontman might be easy to fulfil in this new line-up.

Tanner and Ulrich continued to jam together; the first occasion that Hetfield came along to Newport Beach was also the first time he and Ulrich would be in the same room together. James was, as Tanner remembers, "Thoroughly unimpressed" with Lars's drumming ability at the time, but Ulrich was nothing if not determined, as Hugh recalls. "It did not seem to bother him or faze him that although he was nearly 18 and just learning the drums, that he could not be a rock star in a short order of time. He proclaimed things with such confidence … he sought opportunities [without] even thinking about rejection."

Ulrich only had a small drum kit back then – a fact Kornarens confirmed after an early visit to Ulrich's house: "There was this cupboard in between Lars' and his parents' room. He opens it up and there's a fucking drum-kit in there. The problem was, there was hardly any room for him!"

Driving away from that first session, Tanner clearly remembers what his and Hetfield's initial views of Lars were: "James and I decided Lars was not ready." Hetfield was less complimentary when he told *Playboy* exactly what he thought about his friend's drumming: "Lars had a pretty crappy drum kit, with one cymbal. It kept falling over, and we'd have to stop, and he'd pick the fucking thing up. He really was not a good drummer."

Tanner also believes there were some other issues: "Lars did not seem to fit personality-wise at that time. With James and me, we always seemed to think along the same lines." Ulrich's super-confident self-belief wasn't necessarily seen as a positive at first by Hugh; if anything it was a little unsettling as Tanner admits: "Lars was out of my personal comfort zone."

Whether it fitted or not, Lars Ulrich's implacable belief in where he was going would soon be viewed as a positive, including rather ironically by Tanner himself. Refusing to be discouraged, Ulrich continued with his own agenda, which included an ambitious solo trip to London to hang out with bands like NWOBHM pioneers Diamond Head.

Diamond Head were a British heavy metal band formed in Stourbridge, England in 1976. As one of the original pioneers of the NWOBHM, they had very quickly become an object of considerable adulation for young Ulrich. Although they would struggle to fulfil their early promise, they continue to command some degree of almost mythical respect to this day, largely due to their Metallica connections.

Kornarens remembers an amusing 'Lars moment' during that trip: "So he phones me up after he'd been away for two weeks in London, and tells me he's hanging out with Diamond Head. I say 'No way!' and the next thing he does is put [Diamond Head's singer] Sean Harris on the line." That succinctly summed up Lars's determination, and this unique ability to walk into any situation with a supreme confidence would count for a lot in months to come.

While all this was going on, Brian Slagel was feeding his increasing desire for heavy metal with a job working at Oz Records, which would obviously give him full access to a myriad of imported and other metalage. In addition to that, he was also contributing to *Sounds* magazine back in the UK, and after running into renowned *Kerrang!* scribe Sylvie Simmons, he had also scored some column inches with them – Britain's most popular heavy rock magazine of the era.

As was highlighted before, there was an incredibly vibrant LA music scene at that time, and Slagel definitely felt that the NWOBHM angle was one that more people should really be aware of, so he decided he'd be the one to carry the baton. What that would involve would be the setting up of his own independent record label: Metal Blade Records.

In classic entrepreneurial style, Slagel scratched together money from his own resources and friends (Kornarens would contribute too) with a view to releasing a compilation album of some of the best sounding metal around at that time. Much like all entrepreneurs, Slagel openly admits to "making every mistake humanly possible" in the early days, but his job was made a lot easier by a lawyer friend who worked above Oz Records and who helped the navigation of the legal minefield that is band contracts, royalties and licence agreements etc.

His debut release for the label was to be a compilation album entitled rather grandly *The New Heavy Metal Review Presents Metal Massacre,* and as such would showcase several of the area's hottest bands. When Lars Ulrich heard about it, he was greatly enthused by the whole idea. So much so in fact that he asked Slagel if he could be allowed to submit a song for the record which, given he didn't have a functioning band at the time, was an audacious request, but not in any way out of character. Slagel, unable to resist Ulrich's enthusiasm, agreed.

Another guy Ulrich contacted when he heard about Slagel's idea was James Hetfield, of whom Lars had seen nothing of since that first meeting instigated by Hugh Tanner. He didn't call Hetfield directly though, he used Tanner as the buffer between them, as Hugh recalls: "I hadn't heard much from Lars for six months or so. I got a call at home and recognised that accented voice with a ton of energy on the end of the line. But I was a little reluctant to put him in touch with James because I was aware of James's thoughts on his drumming."

Whatever he thought of Ulrich's drumming, Hetfield was interested in the idea – not to mention the possibility of an actual record deal down the line – so he invited Lars over to the McGovney house to jam.

Hetfield and Ulrich saw each other a lot thereafter and gradually the NWOBHM influences started to rub off on and ultimately replace Hetfield's more traditional tastes – hardly surprising given Ulrich's all-consuming passion for that whole scene, and the amazing connections he'd carved out within it (Lars had befriended Motörhead while they toured the area too).

Kornarens was still seeing a lot of Lars and vividly remembers when James first appeared on his radar. "One day there's a knock on the door and here's Lars with this kid covered in acne." Kornarens remembers Hetfield as quite a shy character then too: "He was quiet and just kind of staring at me. I guess Lars had talked me up. He's got acne and a jeans jacket on with patches of bands like Aerosmith and maybe Ted Nugent."

Once inside, Kornarens and Hetfield talked about the band posters that were on John's bedroom wall, and also acknowledged that they'd both been at the same Aerosmith concert in 1978. Gradually relaxing, Hetfield soon warmed to Kornarens's friendly approach, but from that day forward, Hetfield would see far more of Ulrich than Kornarens.

Significantly too – albeit like many teenagers – James had

discovered alcohol, and Kornarens remembers an incident that occurred on another later visit. "We're sitting on the blue sofa in my parent's sitting room being offered my sister's chocolate chip cookies, and James pulls out some whisky and starts drinking it." Despite being told to stop, Hetfield laughed and continued to swig away from his flask periodically.

Kornarens didn't take long to work out what Hetfield was all about. "I knew his outlet was music. He was not a happy person [then] and he used to drink. And also he didn't really have a job. He had a creative side and he was nice, but he definitely had a dark side about him. He just wasn't ... umm ... perky." Hetfield himself told *Playboy* that, "My mother had just passed away. Everyone was the enemy back then. I wasn't the best at talking ..."

Perky or not, the Hetfield and Ulrich connection was now cementing, and with the looming possibility of forming a band and producing music for an exciting compilation, events would soon start to move very quickly.

CHAPTER 3

"Mettallica"

By 1982, Hetfield, Ulrich and McGovney were spending a lot of time practicing in McGovney's house and occasionally Lars would often stay down there rather than trekking back to Newport Beach every night. It was more or less agreed that Hetfield, Ulrich and McGovney were all behind the idea to lay down a track for Slagel's compilation but they didn't have that much time.

Regardless, Slagel and Kornarens were already going around collecting the fees from bands in the clubs who wanted to appear on it. According to Tanner, a tune that would later morph into 'Hit The Lights' was the one they talked about using, so they needed to record it, and soon. According to Tanner the vibe in the sessions was good and things moved forward significantly: "I had soccer practice one evening but I called in afterwards to see how rehearsals were going and Lars had definitely improved since James last saw him." The problem was that they needed a guitarist, and quickly, in order to get the track down in time for the mastering date.

The reason they were 'short' of a guitarist, was that James at this time was only playing bass and singing, because McGovney – the logical choice for a bassist – hadn't actually committed to joining the band full-time, although the other two were very keen that he did. Lars did have a brief job at a gas station and James also had a fleeting stint at a print shop but neither of them were particularly serious about those roles and were much more into playing music. For that reason, free accommodation was a vital feature in Hetfield's life.

Consequently, Lars placed an advert in the same *Recycler* magazine and a guy called Lloyd Grant replied. Grant was one of the few black, metal guitarists around the LA scene at the time and he remembers getting together with Lars and James: "I answered an ad in the local paper that Lars placed," he told the author. "He auditioned several people and had the ad in there for a while."

Grant was one of numerous neighbourhood people who had responded to the *Recycler* advert; another was musician Joey Allen who ended up as a guitarist in hair-metallers Warrant. Grant continues: "I got busy for a few weeks and then Lars got back in touch and played me James's tape of 'Hit The Lights'. I really liked it and it was the kind of stuff I wanted to do." Grant was also pretty impressed by what he saw in Hetfield: "He was really good. Not quite as he is today but he was still very good. He was very quiet though and seemed quite shy."

Grant seemed to be in pole-position for a permanent spot in the band but there was to be another weird twist given that Lars had left the *Recycler* advert running – Ron McGovney remembers the phone-call that he received as a result: "I took the call and all I remember is this guy on the other end and having to listen to him [talk] about himself. Then I called James to the phone and said, 'Here's another guitar player, but this guy's head won't fit through the door when he gets here.'"

That head in question belonged to Dave Mustaine, who had played with Huntingdon Beach band Panic and had reason to be confident: he was something of a guitar hero with all manner of gear at his disposal. Having at least been in a functioning band, the confident Mustaine not only offered serious shredding ability, but he also brought with him a fair amount of valuable live experience which was something the others did not have at that point.

In all fairness, Grant probably hadn't helped his own cause by sometimes not showing up to rehearsals prior to Mustaine's arrival. He tells the story: "There are so many bands in LA and you never know whether they're going to make it. Also, you have to drive through traffic for rehearsals and I just didn't turn up sometimes. Then Dave came along and got in the band."

So in the end Dave Mustaine did the two lead breaks intended for a version of 'Hit The Lights', but the rest was Hetfield and Ulrich as James told Metal Mike in an interview himself: "We borrowed ourselves a Tascam four-track and recorded 'Hit The Lights'. I played rhythm guitar and bass and sang, while Lars drummed. We were really a duo." Despite Mustaine's two lead solos being perfectly adequate, a version of the second solo recorded by Lloyd Grant literally minutes before the tape was handed over to Slagel, was ultimately the one they decided to go with.

Grant remembers there being no animosity whatsoever after Mustaine replaced him; when I asked Grant the definitive reason for his departure he responded simply: "You'll need to ask James and Lars that question." Grant and Lars still got on well enough to watch the 1982 World Cup Soccer matches together so there was no obvious breakdown in communications, and in fact Grant remains in contact with the band today.

Now that the track was done, all that was needed was to rush the thing over to Slagel so that it could be mastered from reel-to-reel tape at Bijou Studios in Hollywood. There was a problem, however, and that was that Lars's recording was on audio-cassette which needed to be transferred, and this would cost money.

John Kornarens remembers the tape hand-over vividly. "The tape was due at 3pm, and Brian and I are standing outside on the sidewalk and this was busy Hollywood. Lars then comes running up all out of breath and pulls this cassette from his back pocket."

What Lars didn't know was that to convert the cassette to reel tape was going to cost fifty dollars and that was something he did not have. "Lars's head all of a sudden turns to me and he says, 'Do you have fifty bucks?' Fortunately I had fifty-two bucks sitting in there, which I gave to him. I never got it back either!" laughs Kornarens.

While Slagel's compilation was being finished, and the cover printed etc, there were further developments within the band. James had used Ron McGovney's bass to record the bass parts for 'Hit The Lights' but McGovney still wasn't that keen on being a full-time band member. "I was more interested in going to see Mötley Crüe at the clubs", McGovney admits. "Then one night we're sitting having a few beers and I start to play the bass part for 'Hit The Lights' and James, Lars and Dave join in. Maybe it was my drunkenness, or even my awe at Dave's guitar playing that made me finally agree to join."

When the track appeared on the first pressing of the *Metal Massacre* compilation, Metallica finally had a vinyl presence, and this rather unusually preceded any recognised demo of their own. Amusingly, the first pressing of the vinyl album had a few spelling errors including Lloyd Grant's name and unbelievably the band title itself which read 'Mettallica'. That first edition remains a true collector's item, while future pressings saw the bewildering errors being corrected.

Incidentally, that exact origin of that band name has been the subject of considerable debate over the years. Hugh Tanner remembers hearing it from Lars and not being initially thrilled by it. "Honestly, like most names ... I did not like it at first. No one else argued and it just came to pass. James had a draft board from his high school days and it was set up in Ron's house. James had already designed the Metallica logo on it which is the logo exactly as it stands today."

Ron Quintana, the editor of a metal fanzine from San Francisco, and a long-time friend of the band, had asked Ulrich which of two names, 'Metallica' or 'Metal Mania' sounded better for his fanzine. The choice of the Metallica name was ultimately taken for the band. Hetfield's early artistic ability which had been shrewdly identified years ago by McGovney turned out to be invaluable after all, as that logo is one of the most effective and recognisable images in music history. Although the band would abandon it for a while on a few mid-1990s album covers, the logo has remained largely the same to this day.

Another guy who recognised Hetfield's early talent was Katon de Pena, who at that time was playing in various Orange County bands, but would later form his own outfit called Hirax. He remembers seeing the logo and was clearly impressed. "James was extremely talented. Not just musically but artistically as well. I remember he showed me that hand drawn logo and I remember thinking, 'If this guy doesn't make it as a musician, he'll definitely make it as an artist.'" It wasn't just the band logo either, as Katon remembers: "He was always wearing t-shirts with all the newest kick-ass bands. One time he turned up in a Saxon *Strong Arm Of The Law* shirt which he made and it was so good I was sure he must have got it from the Saxon fan-club, but he made it himself."

De Pena also confirms how initially reserved but ultimately likeable James was at the time. "James was quiet, but once you got to know him he was great fun to hang out with. If you were into the same kind of music he was into ... you could talk and get drunk for many, many hours! We all used to hang out together, and do a bit of smoking and drinking. We'd always somehow end up listening to Diamond Head, Venom and Saxon albums. We'd rage all night until the sun came up, but every time, James would be the last one standing!"

So, with a name as well as a feisty presence on a new compilation album, the band – with a seemingly settled line-up – would start to investigate the possibility of playing some live shows themselves on the LA club circuit. What was still uncertain at this point was whether James was destined to be the band's full-time singer – a fact which seems incredible nowadays when you consider how effective he has become.

Sammy DeJohn was an LA singer and his path crossed with James during this period. "A couple of my friends were going to Hollywood to this little dive to see a band," Sammy remembers. "They said I needed to see them. So we got to this bar and James is standing outside so we walked up and started talking to him. He had this bottle of vodka so we took a couple of shots of that, and he told me they were looking for a singer."

So it seems that James was keen to distance himself from vocal duties, even though the first song was out and being well received. "I ended up going down to their place to rehearse as their singer, and that lasted maybe a few weeks," Sammy recalls. "But it never happened and I really don't think that Mustaine liked me at all." Despite the coalition not amounting to anything permanent, DeJohn recognised James's talent for sure. "I thought James was really cool and we got along real well. As a musician, it's his voice and the way he totally commands the stage that makes him what he is."

Meanwhile, the band members were regularly seen in and around the LA club scene as spectators, and Bob Nalbandian, who ran a metal radio show in the area, particularly remembers noticing James. "I saw him around the time they formed and it was outside the Woodstock Club in Anaheim. There were two clubs next door to each other – Woodstock and Radio City." Nalbandian was himself a regular on the rock and metal club scene back then and would turn up at the venues to see whoever was playing. "I would always see James at these shows and I never knew who he was. I used to have a jacket with Motörhead and Saxon patches on it and I'd always see James and he would just stare at my jacket."

Despite clearly noticing Nalbandian and being intrigued by his clothing, Hetfield would rarely actually speak as Bob remembers: "He had a Motörhead shirt on back then and I was too shy to go up and talk to him either." Nalbandian had another friend called Pat Scott who had previously met Lars when he too responded to that famous *Recycler* ad, and that connection in turn brought Lars into Nalbandian's world.

After a visit to Lars's house that involved raking through what Nalbandian described as "the ultimate record collection", he asked Scott if Lars was in a band. Scott replied, "Yeah, you know that guy we always see at the Woodstock with the Motörhead shirt? Well, he's the singer."

After that revelation, Nalbandian ran into Hetfield again at the Woodstock and this time they connected properly, as Bob remembers: "Finally he came up and I said, 'Hey! You're singing with that band Metallica right?' and he freaked out and said, 'Wow, how do you know?' and then, 'Someone recognised me! We haven't even played a gig yet!' We started talking a bit and he was a really, really nice guy. He was real shy and quiet."

From that point on, the two just rapped about metal and all the cool bands in LA, not to mention Lars's amazing record collection. "Lars was always the real driven one. Back in the day James was real quiet and reserved," Nalbandian confirms. "And the next time I would hang out with James would be after the band's first ever show at Radio City."

That legendary first live performance would indeed take place at Radio City on March 14, 1982, and from all reports, it was a total disaster. Nalbandian was there – as he was at all their early shows – and right from the get-go things went hideously wrong as he explains: "It was horrible. Dave's guitar string broke and they didn't have a back-up guitar, so in the middle of the set they had to re-string it." Hardly a memorable first appearance and Nalbandian remembers the set-list being pretty limited too. "They did just covers at the time and the only original was 'Hit The Lights' and maybe one other."

That disastrous debut didn't appear to put the band off though as Nalbandian recalls what Lars told him after the show: "Lars said, 'Yeah we're going to open up for Saxon in a couple of weeks' and I said, 'Fuck you, you're full of shit, you'll never open for Saxon!' But they *did* get that show." That show opening for Saxon at the Whisky actually came about on the back of McGovney's photography connections. His hard work and persistence put him in touch with the venue's booking agent, although this second gig was apparently only a marginal improvement on their live initiation.

Bob remembers distinctly how James behaved that night too. "He was still very shy and he didn't talk to the audience at all. And you have to remember that he was only singing back then. It was only their second gig and man did it show."

Jim Durkin, a former pupil of Downey High School, was a few years younger than James. Durkin was very much an aspiring metal-head in those days, and would eventually become part of the influential thrash outfit Dark Angel. He also found himself at those early gigs as he fondly recalls: "I'm not gonna say I was an old friend or anything, and hung out all the time," Jim confesses, "but I was at all the gigs, and would go up and talk to James and Lars and ask questions – being the fan-boy I was. James gave me a Metallica button, which I still have."

Durkin had been learning guitar in his last year at high school, and he already thought he knew a lot before he even saw the band play. "At the time I thought I knew what metal was. Then I met Dave Marrs, and he told me to go and see Metallica. I was blown away. It changed my life."

Hugh Tanner was still loosely involved with the band in an assisting capacity. Consequently, he was sniffing around trying to book live shows, recording time, or anything else that would enhance the band's reputation. Tanner remembers how confident Lars was about his band making it big, particularly during one typically highly charged phonecall: "We are going to be the world's greatest band and you are going to be the world's greatest manager," Ulrich yelled down the phone, and he discussed the management company, and two names which it could be called: "Metal Up Your Ass Productions or Thunderfuck Productions," Tanner remembers.

While Tanner would soon bow out of the story, his role in the early life of James Hetfield – and by association the band that would become Metallica – is very important. Talking about his role now – having been silent for so long – Tanner is keen that it should be an inspiration for young aspiring musicians (which it clearly is). "I have a desire to tell the story to speak to aspiring bands and musicians. All that I said was with the perspective of a high school kid longing to be a rock star. If this is you, then to you I dedicate my long standing silence, and wish you great success in your endeavours."

With or without an official management company but keen to advertise themselves more following their early live exposure, the band elected to put together a small four-track demo on a slightly more professional level. This demo cassette consisted of: 'Hit The Lights', 'Motorbreath', 'Jump In The Fire' and a fourth track called 'Mechanix' – which had been given a live airing at one of the band's early live shows. The resulting tape became known as *The Power Metal Demo*. That wasn't intentional though, and in fact only happened because Ron McGovney had added the words 'Power Metal' under the band's logo when he handed it out with flyers to club promoters in the area.

The Power Metal Demo would be a stepping-stone to the band's first full demo entitled *No Life 'til Leather* (the opening line of 'Hit The Lights'), wherein added to it were three newer songs: 'Seek And Destroy', 'Metal Militia' and 'Phantom Lord'.

Katon de Pena, who was still part of James's social circle at the time, remembers his first exposure to the demo. "James made me sit down with old-school headphones and listen to it." He wouldn't be the only one that would be compelled to hear this demo, if James got his way.

After raising some cash and experiencing a few initial creative differences with producer Kenny Kane (a connection of Hugh Tanner's making) who had more of a punk reputation, the demo eventually got recorded to everyone's satisfaction in a studio in Orange County. When it was released it proceeded to spread like a rash – even as far afield as Japan. Of more immediate significance though was the rabid reception closer to home, and the reaction of a metal scene screaming out for something new.

One town where it landed with huge impact was San Francisco, and this degree of interest from LA's rival city six hours drive up the coast would become even more significant as time passed. And why did this demo make such a massive impact? The presence of that distinctive crunch in Hetfield's guitar sound even in these early days really should have been forewarning of what was to follow.

With his precise and distinctive palm-muted picking, Hetfield had discovered a guitar sound that nobody had really heard before, and certainly nobody had heard it honed to this degree of precision and frightening power. For those not familiar with that term, palm-muting is the practice of using the picking hand (in this case the right), to dampen the sound and not let it resonate. This gave metal riffs a new kind of blunt-force power, and young Hetfield was an early master of it.

Arguably, this was the beginning of thrash metal as we know it. Less palatable – and for that matter recognisable – was the vocal delivery, which at that time had a far more annoyingly lightweight sound than the latterday iconic Hetfield. He was attempting to sing rather more here than the clipped, barked delivery he'd so famously adopt in future years. Sadly, James used very limited melody or harmony in these early days, so the vocals came across rather immaturely at times. What James lacked vocally, he more than made up for with his guitar.

Jim Durkin, who was continuing to develop his own guitar playing, rates Hetfield among the greats. "Iommi invented the heavy sound, but James invented the thrash sound. Palm-muted and tight riffing. He was the law!"

Metallica continued to play around the LA area, mixing with bands like Ratt and Stryper with whom they actually had zero in common in terms of sound or ideology. That was until their friend Brian Slagel called and asked if the band would play on a bill he had assembled called *Metal Massacre Night* that would air at the

Keystone in San Francisco on September 18, 1982. It was only because another band Cirith Ungol had dropped out that Metallica even got that call, and that twist of fate would forever alter the destiny of the band.

However, while things seemed to be rolling along just nicely, there were a few differences starting to surface among the band members, with Ron McGovney feeling the pinch most. Whatever happened, and all band's histories are thick with rumours, it's almost certain that Ron felt that his help, accommodation and general good nature was not fully appreciated by the other three. This issue would slowly start to cause serious internal band conflict.

So, when the time came to travel up to San Francisco, the ever-dependable Ron McGovney used his dad's 1969 Ford Ranger to haul all the gear and his band-mates up the coast to a city he did not know his way around. He later told *Shockwaves* magazine that seeing his partying band-mates in the back of the van did little to relieve his general dissatisfaction.

However, something that must have softened the blow was the completely rabid response that greeted Metallica that night. Anyone who was there – and there were seemingly only 200 bodies in the place – said it was like a bomb had been dropped, and as Ron told KNAC it was all something of an eye-opener. "We had no idea our *No Life' til Leather* demo had gotten up there; they knew all the lyrics to our songs and everything." It seemed that unlike in LA, the Bay Area crowd really understood where the band was coming from and were vocal in their support, as McGovney realised: "It was a trip, we couldn't believe it. When we played in LA with bands like Ratt, people would just stand there with their arms crossed."

Brian Slagel remembers how shy James still was, even on that journey to San Francisco. "We all kind of travelled up together and stayed in the same hotel on that trip. He was still super shy, and he wasn't the kind of guy that you go and hang out with for hours on end and talk to him," Slagel laughs. "He was super-cool though, and obviously the more he drank, the more his personality came out in those days."

Despite that fantastic show in San Francisco, in general, Ron

McGovney's position in the band was becoming precarious for various reasons, some of them personal, and his days in Metallica were by now distinctly numbered. "I was starting to feel alienated from the band. It was them, and then there was me, "McGovney concedes sadly. It was obvious that relations were broken irreparably and at this point, the band actively began looking for a new bass player.

The McGovney situation was brought to the attention of Brian Slagel when they next got together in LA and Slagel's suggestion was that the band should go and check out a Bay Area band called Trauma, whom he had seen at the Whisky in LA a few weeks previously. It wasn't to see Trauma *per se* (although they would get a slot on the second *Metal Massacre* compilation) but they did have a bass player of astounding virtuosity and on-stage aura, and his name was Cliff Burton.

Not only was he supremely gifted, but Burton had a presence on-stage that resembled some kind of musical whirlwind, and as such he was a talent that just couldn't be ignored, in Slagel's educated opinion. Ron McGovney remembers seeing Burton play with the others, and views that night as something of a death sentence for him in the band. "I remember saying to James: 'That bass player is playing the lead!' He and Lars were mesmerised. I thought: 'Oh no, here is the end.'"

Never one to miss an opportunity, Lars approached Burton after the show with an offer to join the band, and was surprised when Burton initially declined because of his general indifference for LA. Nevertheless, the contact was made and from that day on, Cliff Burton was always going to be the next Metallica bass player.

Although there was all this ongoing upheaval, the band continued to honour live performances despite a continuing feeling that Metallica still never actually went down that well in LA, a city populated by crowds who were much more receptive to glam and hair metal. Thrash was just starting to catch on in LA, ironically, when Metallica were about to leave, as Jim Durkin remembers: "At the start there were no bands anywhere near that sound in LA. Then all of a sudden, bands started popping up all over LA, doing their own take on things – including Dark Angel."

Durkin isn't totally convinced that Metallica invented thrash however: "Metallica opened the door, opened eyes. There was more to the local metal scene than just being the next Maiden, Priest or Sabbath. Did they invent thrash? No, that sound was defined by *all* the bands to come, but Metallica certainly set the standard." Despite his declining Lars's earlier offer, Burton remained in the picture and even appeared in the audience at a Metallica show at the Old Waldorf in October where the band's performance actually went down really well – at least by LA standards.

November 11 saw another breakthrough performance at the Woodstock in Anaheim, where they supported journeyman metal act of the day Y & T, and Nalbandian remembers the significant impact of James playing second guitar that night: "It really beefed up their sound and that was a turning point where I thought, 'Wow, this band could really do something', because until then they had never really gone down that well."

The next two shows the band played would be vitally important for a whole host of reasons. The first of them was on November 29 at the Old Waldorf, and it was significant because it was recorded for live demo purposes and released under the name of *Live Metal Up Your Ass*.

Due to problems with the venue's mixing board, that night's show was recorded via a cassette recorder placed in front of the PA, and the final sound quality was predictably hideous. The second reason was the support band were an up-and-coming Bay Area band called Exodus whose guitarist was a shy 20-year-old called Kirk Hammett – more of him later.

The next night Metallica played their second show in San Francisco at the Mabuhay Gardens, and this would be notable for the simple reason that it would be the last time Ron McGovney played with the band. Apparently, the return journey down the coast was a hideous culmination of everything that was bad about his and his colleague's relationship, and McGovney had simply had enough. McGovney remembers it all well: "Cliff was at that gig in San Francisco and for me the writing was on the wall. So when we got back to LA, I quit." Further friction between Ron and Dave Mustaine exacerbated matters and McGovney then kicked everyone out of his house.

Burton finally agreed to join the band after his initial reservations. Burton was a thoughtful character and a man of considerable wisdom for his years. While he was fond of partying, he certainly wasn't boisterous or loud. What he did possess however was a wealth of talent and an implacable will for where it might take him. It was that drive and desire to broaden his and his band's musical horizons that would quickly become a valuable addition to the tapestry of Metallica.

Admirably McGovney is pretty philosophical about those times nowadays, and admits that the band was not everything for him: "I admit I spent more time with my girlfriend than with those other guys. This was my first girlfriend, you know, a hot chick to spend quality time with. I also missed a few band practices to go and see Mötley Crüe gigs and they didn't like that at all."

What is totally certain is that without Ron McGovney, the James Hetfield story would have been very different indeed. After all, without free board and a place to practice, James Hetfield's adolescent life may well have progressed very differently. Bob Nalbandian probably sums it up as well as anyone. "I always say this about Ron: he was an integral part of the early days of Metallica."

Ron himself looks at it all a little more modestly. "I think they would have found a way. I think that Lars can talk anyone into anything. He is just so persistent and they definitely had the drive and talent to make it without my financial support." A classy sign-off from a classy guy, and at this point Ron McGovney departs the James Hetfield story as a hugely important factor. At the same time, Metallica would soon depart from an ungrateful Los Angeles for the receptive warmth of San Francisco.

Chapter 4

The Metallica Mansion

After all the drama of Ron McGovney's departure, Hetfield, Ulrich and Mustaine now had a problem as to how to move all their belongings to San Francisco, a process that ultimately took almost four months to complete. In fact, it wouldn't be until late March of 1983 that James and Lars took up residence at a property at 3132 Carlson Boulevard, El Cerrito, which belonged to a friend of theirs called Mark Whitaker. The condition of that apartment was apparently a little run-down, and the neighbourhood itself probably not one of the area's best, so the residence inherited the rather ironic nickname The Metallica Mansion.

Ron Quintana was invited to a few of the many early parties that took place at the Mansion: "James was very gruff. Very withdrawn and hidden," Ron remembers. "Until he drank, then he'd kind of come out of his shell." At that time, Whitaker was training to become a sound engineer as well as managing the exciting Bay Area band Exodus with whom Metallica had played a show back in LA at the tail-end of 1982. Mustaine, unlike the other two, ended up taking a room at Whitaker's grandmother's house, which must have been a strange mixture particularly for the latter – but it seemed to work. Although it took a while, the move north was worth doing as James told *Thrasher* magazine himself in1986: "Now that I think of it ... it was really wild that we did that. All of a sudden, we just move up to SF, no place to stay or nothing. It was cool!"

In the early 1980s, the Bay Area was a fast evolving vibrant metal scene and consequently all the musicians were very tight, which meant they all congregated at the same gigs and parties. The main players in the early days were Metallica and local residents Exodus, but there was a whole host of other bands like Death Angel and

Possessed also on the rise – spurred on by an energy and atmosphere that suggested something serious was in the air.

It wasn't a big scene geographically though, and in reality, the San Francisco club circuit revolved around venues like Ruthie's Inn, The Waldorf, the Stone and Mabuhay Gardens. However, what they lacked in size and number, the clubs more than made up for in energy as these sweaty venues seemed to inhale the sound that these bands emitted; on any given night you could see four or five killer bands perform on the same bill.

Somebody who ran into James after one of these shows at the Stone was a Bay Area resident by the name of Fred Cotton, a guy who Hetfield would have a lot in common with, and somebody who'd consequently become an important ally for several years. Fred recalls hooking up: "We went to a party back at Mark Whitaker's and we totally hit it off. He had a presence about him definitely, but I had no idea at that time that he'd become what he did. At that time, he just looked like someone you'd want to hang out and identify with." Cotton also noticed that something was going on with the Bay Area music scene. "At the time; they were *it*. That was the shit. I mean I was floored. James really connected with the people through the music just by being himself. The music back then was so amazing – all you could do was just bow."

This was a new movement for sure, but the area had always been receptive to metal apparently. Eric Peterson, who actually founded Legacy (Testament's early incarnation), grew up in the Bay Area and remembers his teenage experiences fondly. "When I was 15 or 16," he told writer Joel McIver, "the Bay Area had this thing called 'Day On The Green' at the outdoor Coliseum. Every summer we had two of them. My first concert was Ted Nugent, Aerosmith, AC/DC with Bon Scott and Mahogany Rush."

A future band-mate of Peterson's, who was also around the scene at the time, was Chuck Billy. Chuck would become the singer in the fully-fledged Testament, and they were a band who followed very much in the Metallica slipstream having released their first and arguably best record confusingly entitled *The Legacy* in 1987. Although they wouldn't achieve the vast cross-spectrum commercial success that Metallica would, they remain to this day an important genre pioneer.

Chuck's a larger than life character in all senses, and one of the most respected guys in this business, and he vividly remembers James in the early days in San Francisco. "Metallica actually bonded that scene together even tighter. James was always the guy who was just real and never beat around the bush. He was kind of loud and outspoken back then with a little more drinking and partying than nowadays maybe," Billy continues. "So it was a different James back then."

It seems that the presence of Metallica was definitely a unifying factor for the Bay Area thrash scene and the band did their part to support other acts who were fighting to make their way too, as Billy recalls: "When we started, James and the other guys would always come down to our shows and that was a big highlight for us. And it also made us be on our toes!"

Ron Quintana, who was running a radio station at the time, remembers that James used to occasionally guest DJ on his show around this time, with mixed results: "They would come up and guest DJ, or instead come on and be drunk and swear – getting me in trouble!" It certainly wasn't all about partying for Metallica though, and with Cliff Burton now fully on board, they set about capitalising on the excitement that their *No Life 'til Leather* demo had started, by building on an already excellent live reputation. Many early witnesses opine that the Metallica sound was given a completely new dimension with Burton's classically trained playing, and the live Metallica experience certainly benefitted from his energetic stage presence.

At one gig at the Stone in the spring of 1983, the band added some new and more complex features to their live experience, most notably a Burton bass solo called 'Anesthesia' along with a couple of new and reworked songs.

The west coast of the country wasn't the only place that the Metallica effect was beginning to be felt however; three time zones away in New York, a cassette of that roughly recorded *Live Metal Up Your Ass* demo had found its way into the hands of an artist manager and record store entrepreneur called Jon Zazula, nicknamed Jonny 'Z'.

Zazula had a famous record store called Rock 'n' Roll Heaven, which was located in East Brunswick, NJ. In addition, both he and his wife Marsha managed bands under the name Crazed Management, and they were both renowned for their ability to spot new talent and develop it to maximum commercial effect. In fact, their foresight and considerable persistence had successfully introduced metal bands like Anvil and Venom to an American audience.

Not just that, Jonny himself was a real extrovert who'd throw everything into every project with total enthusiasm and determination. What the Zazulas both saw in the Metallica sound – even through the thick fog of that live demo – was an energy and newness, which in their view blended the sound of bands like Motörhead and the NWOBHM, with something very American. And this, in their eyes, was an innovative, lethal, and not to mention potentially lucrative mixture.

Zazula remembers first hearing the demo: "Somebody brought the demo into the store and it blew my mind. I thought this was the greatest thing since white bread. Marsha and I had twelve shows going on at the time with bands like Twisted Sister and we thought it would be cool to bring them [Metallica] over and give them a shot."

Suitably impressed by what they had heard, the Zazulas got word to Lars Ulrich that they'd like the band to come to New York to play the shows and talk about some business ideas. Fortunately, Lars was well aware of the Zazulas' reputation for being shrewd judges of talent, so he agreed to travel over with the band and see what came of it.

The only problem with that arrangement was that the band didn't have any money. Zazula sent them $1500 towards the cost of the trip. "To me [that] was like a million dollars back then." The band, accompanied by Whitaker, then hired a U-Haul van and a truck with a view to driving the huge mileage to the East Coast.

What occurred on that 3000-mile journey across America was to become infamous. The close confines of a long distance journey together quickly brought matters to a head. As the rumours go, James and Lars had already made the decision to kick Mustaine out of the band at a point "somewhere between Chicago and

Idaho", but it transpired that they did not do it officially until they got to the east coast.

Zazula remembers the band arriving at his home: "When they got to my house, two of them had been in the back of the truck the whole ride with the gear, and the other three were in the front." Zazula was surprised by what happened next, "The first thing they did after 'hello' was to raid my liquor cabinet!"

What became apparent when the band landed on Zazula's doorstep was that they didn't actually have anywhere to go. "They had nothing except the gear and the clothes on their back," Zazula confirms. For the first part of their time in New York, the band continued to stay at the Zazula's house as guests, until such a time as an alternative was available.

Although Mustaine hadn't officially left yet, the band was not without a contingency plan to replace him, and the person they had in mind was Exodus guitarist Kirk Hammett. Obviously they'd become aware of his ability through the San Francisco metal circles, and also Mark Whitaker looked after Hammett's band so there was an obvious and open channel of communication.

Meanwhile in New York, the band played two live shows on April 8 and 9 supporting Vandenberg and the Rods respectively, then after a day off they packed Mustaine's bags for him while Hetfield told him he was no longer in the band. As the story goes, there was very little discussion or ceremony, and Mustaine was apparently on a Greyhound bus back to San Francisco one hour later. Whatever the reasons, Dave Marrs believes Mustaine would have been fired at another point in the future: "I just don't think they ever would have got along, I really don't." The Metallica vs Mustaine debate rumbled on for years, and if anything, James Hetfield probably commented least about it of all the band members. To this day, it is still a subject that fans of Metallica regularly bring up. Whatever the Metallica issues, Dave Mustaine would go on to form Megadeth – themselves a monster act in their own right. Throughout their extremely successful career, Mustaine and his band would contribute hugely to the overall fabric of rock music, with their 1990 album *Rust In Peace* considered by many experts to be one of the best technical metal albums of the modern era.

The bottom line though was a call was put in to Kirk Hammett asking him to fly immediately to New York to audition for a spot in Metallica. As it happened, the timing of that call was actually very good because firstly, Hammett liked what he had seen of Metallica, and secondly he was a little frustrated with his own band Exodus's lack of progress. Therefore, it suited both parties and despite Hammett thinking that the initial call was a hoax, he flew to New York and started jamming with Hetfield, Ulrich and Burton.

Hammett turned up, played brilliantly and so was in the band – and therefore remained in New York. Apart from anything else, the band didn't have any money to fly him back, so having been absorbed into Metallica like rock music's version of osmosis, Kirk Hammett made his live debut with the band on April 16 at the Showplace in New Jersey.

Metallica continued to party hard at the Zazula residence, to the point that John and Marsha decided that they should go elsewhere, and found them accommodation in a place called The Music Building in Queens, New York. That arrangement would have been fine if there had been any rooms left, as Zazula recalls: "We found them a terrible place! They were living in squalor at the top of the building where all the garbage was kept. Things like old desks and chairs were in there instead of being thrown out in the street." Also using that building was New York thrash band Anthrax, who were from Queens themselves, and had a room set up there to rehearse.

Anthrax were to become the East Coast wing of the so-called 'Big Four' of thrash bands, with the other three being Megadeth, Slayer and of course Metallica. Their career ran fairly parallel to that of Metallica until the early 1990s, thereafter Metallica's ascent into rock superstardom coincided with Anthrax's gradual slide into relative low-profile – for a whole host of reasons that aren't relevant here. What is relevant is that the bands were very close in those early days. Anthrax's drummer Charlie Benante remembers when James and the boys showed up. "I met James for the first time at our rehearsal studio and that's where the friendship started. For me, I bonded most with Kirk at first. James was kind of quiet in the beginning. I always felt in the early days that James was quite unapproachable. And then once the surface stuff was finished, we could kind of hang and talk about shit."

Benante confirms an impression of Hetfield that most people from that early era seem to share, and it appears that it always took a while for his defences to come down. Maybe it was shyness, or maybe it was a general mistrust of people generally that dated back to his childhood in Downey. Either way, Hetfield was certainly a tough nut to crack as even the effusive Zazula admits. "It took a bit to get to talk to him personally from what I remember. You had to catch James at the right moment. He seemed in those days to carry a lot of ghosts, and he certainly didn't like to discuss them. But I guess if you want to get personal with a person, you ask those questions but he wasn't so quick to give up the answers." That succinct synopsis of the Hetfield psyche was probably as good a marker as any for where he was aged 20, and Zazula's references to 'ghosts' must surely refer to the pain and lack of understanding James was still carrying from his parent's sudden divorce, and his mother's premature death.

Moreover, James was becoming increasingly dominant in the line-up. What had started in 1983 was a pattern of behaviour that would be repeated throughout his career. To understand, you have to categorise Metallica's band members at that time. You had two quiet and relatively mild figures in Hammett and Burton. Then you had the vocally confident and super-energetic Ulrich, and then there was the passively controlling spectre of Hetfield – in many ways the wolf at the other's door. This triangle of power and control probably started when Hammett joined, and consequently this era – prior to any full album being released – was the beginning of many years of this kind of tension, which at times was highly creative, and at others threatened to destroy the band itself.

For the time being, the positives of being under the Zazulas' wing were clearly obvious, given that the next live commitments organised were an act of genius on Jonny's part. Due to the connections he had in both his home country and abroad, Zazula decided that a bill pairing Metallica with legendary British black metal pioneers Venom was a good idea. In some ways he was right because the two shows the bands played at the Paramount in

Staten Island on April 22 and April 24, 1983, will go down in metal history, albeit for not entirely the right reasons.

At that time, observers would definitely pitch Venom in at the evil end of the metal spectrum, and with two well-received albums and a reputation for insane live shows, they were a few significant steps ahead of Metallica. Like Metallica previously, Venom had been invited to reside at the Zazula house ahead of the shows. What actually went on is probably best left to the imagination, but it seems certain that on one occasion the Zazula's kitchen nearly caught fire after a late night cooking attempt!

They didn't reserve their fire-raising exploits for Zazula's kitchen either, given that they almost destroyed the Paramount on the first night after an over-ambitious pyrotechnic display. Hetfield himself got caught up in the excitement of those Venom shows, and it cost him a trip to hospital to treat six stitches in his hand after falling while holding a vodka bottle.

Despite all the drama, the combination of Metallica and their heroes Venom on the same bill was considered a complete success by all concerned, particularly James and Lars, who told a KUSF interviewer: "We might do something with Venom if they can get off their ass and do more than one album every five years."

Speaking of albums, Zazula – after seeing the potential that Metallica offered – was already giving considerable thought to finding a way of recording a debut Metallica album. Although he was not officially their manager, Zazula had taken on kind of a surrogate role that worked for both parties, and in any case, the band at that time had no viable alternatives back in San Francisco.

There were however two problems. Firstly, no record companies particularly gave a damn about being involved with Metallica at that time, and certainly had no desire to take what would be a commercial flyer on a relatively extreme act. Secondly, even if a company had fancied a piece of Metallica, the band had absolutely no financial muscle whatsoever, which meant that any album deal would need to be done on a fairly minimal budget, to put it mildly.

What the Zazula's decided to do next would turn out to be jointly one of the most risky and yet shrewd decisions in rock history. "We decided that we should fund the whole damn thing

ourselves. The recording, the manufacturing, everything."
  And that is exactly what they did.

Chapter 5

Kill 'Em All

Manoeuvring a wild animal like Metallica into a position to record a debut album is an achievement that should never be underestimated, especially given the minimal resources that were available. The Zazulas had just had a child too, and to put themselves 'out there' financially was an extremely risky proposition. To pull it off, they needed everything to fall right, and so fortunately – due to their busy touring schedule – the band were in good shape to proficiently lay down tracks in a studio situation. Just as well given that that the Zazulas simply couldn't afford them much time to get it done.

Anthrax's Charlie Benante, having seen Hetfield sing first-hand, knew that his strengths would make the forthcoming recording a fruitful exercise. "James just went up there and said, 'This is how I'm going sing, you can either love it or hate it.' Luckily for him, it went well with the music. Just like Lemmy goes well with Motörhead's music."

None of this uncertainty particularly worried Zazula however, as his determined approach had already hooked him up with a recording studio in upstate New York called Barren Alley, which by the time Metallica turned up there during the first week in May was called simply Music America.

Zazula remembers it being easily the best option available: "It had a really good sound board and there was a good space where you could crash. It was a good, clean, big studio and Manowar had just recorded there. Manowar sounded really good to us for those days, and we're talking about *Into Glory Ride*, not the other album."

So Zazula had found a recording space, and he had also uncovered a sound engineer there called Chris Bubacz who "seemed to get it". Also available was a guy called Paul Curcio, and he would be given the unenviable task of trying to commit Metallica's live sound faithfully to vinyl for the first time.

"Paul was a big guitar guy, and I believe he worked on some of the early Santana albums. He really understood the guitar, although he didn't really understand the heaviness of [Metallica]," Zazula explains. Curcio was quickly educated as to what the band wanted however, and in a matter of a couple of weeks an album of ten tracks was recorded.

Zazula particularly remembers a unique ability of Hetfield's during that recording process. "I thought of James as an artist with a talent. Except his way of painting was by heavying songs up. On one occasion while we were recording [the debut album] *Kill 'Em All*, James came up to me and said, 'Hey, do I get to heavy my album up yet?'" Apparently when the album was being recorded initially, it had a lot of high-end guitar and was distinctly lightweight in sound, that was until James was asked to go back into the studio and change that.

As far as the actual title was concerned, the original idea James and the band had was to name the record *Metal Up Your Ass*, but Zazula and the distribution company felt that something so direct and visceral (the cover would have an image of a sword emerging from a toilet bowl) just wouldn't fly in a cautiously minded music business at that time. The band didn't like that prudent approach, and as the story goes, Cliff Burton suggested the title *Kill 'Em All* in reference to what he'd like to do to record label types – and everyone immediately agreed.

The album cover itself was something of a blunt statement of intent too, depicting a large, heavy-looking hammer, a pool of blood, and the ominous shadow of the hand that was presumably wielding the hammer. It was 'no nonsense', and as such was entirely representative of the record's contents.

The completed album consisted of ten tracks, all of which had appeared in a live environment at some point during the previous year. Some of them dated back even further. Whatever their age, it was a potent selection of songs, and more importantly it sounded like nothing else out there. While the recording process was largely a successful one in that the result was a stunning debut release, there is some debate as to whether the band were happy with how much help they actually got during the two weeks it took to lay the album down.

Zazula – given it was his baby, is understandably defensive: "Paul Curcio was definitely told what was required and I don't remember James complaining." Hetfield himself was a lot more direct when asked about the sessions by *Thrasher* magazine in 1986, where he was openly critical of Curcio.

So, what of the album itself? To try and critically assess a record that is intrinsic to the very fabric of what we know as heavy metal, is like a modern art critic attempting to sensibly appraise *The Mona Lisa* – no easy job. With that proviso in mind, the record fades straight in to 'Hit The Lights', which had been kicking around in some form or another for five years or more. Having said that, this version of it was a far more streamlined beast, which really illustrated how far the new line-up had come since those early demos. What is also immediately apparent is the utter precision and speed of Hetfield's rhythm attack – which of course is the key to music played at this velocity being effective. Vocally he's a million miles away from his latterday fully-formed self and at times his delivery comes over as still rather immature. But as a lead off track it's a stunning declaration of intent.

'The Four Horsemen' follows, and in many ways it's several years ahead of its time in structure. Given that in later years the band would develop a knack for progressive compositions that moved seamlessly through different tempos while never sacrificing anything in the way of heaviness, this was something of a surprise. With its scrabbling intro riff which eases smoothly into a mid-tempo chug, this is considerably more complicated than most of its siblings. Listen out carefully for Burton's always-expansive bass lines that continually serve to add colour to Hetfield's brutally disciplined rhythm regime.

If there's a weakness on *Kill 'Em All* (it's hard to sling any kind of criticism at one of metal's most vital debuts), then it surely must be 'Jump In The Fire'. With a riff that's just too cheerful for its own good, it doesn't sit well stylistically with anything else on the record. It's overtly commercial with an almost sing-a-long chorus and despite being well constructed, goes very much against the thrash metal grain.

The next sound on the record are the eternal words of James Hetfield quietly announcing what's next: "Bass solo, take one". What follows is one of the most astounding exhibitions of instrumental virtuosity on record, yet one that at no point descends into pointless self-indulgence on the part of bassist Cliff Burton. Called simply 'Anesthesia (Pulling Teeth)', it's a four-minute ascent into some kind of bass guitar outer space, featuring all manner of classical patterns – simply stunning.

After that bewildering interlude, the listener is forced to re-enter earth's orbit courtesy of the completely uncompromising 'Whiplash', which for many is *Kill 'Em All*'s centrepiece. It's lyrically mindless of course, just an ode to the art of head banging, but musically it's a headlong, furious charge into metal history. Considering that it is regularly cited as the first real thrash metal song ever, few would question its worth on any level.

'Phantom Lord' is next, and as we've heard already, it's a song which had been kicking around rehearsal rooms for years too – as well as being the name of one of Hetfield's early bands. It's a slippery riff actually, which then grinds down into a brief and rather atmospheric mid-song breather before Hammett dials in one of his more crafted lead breaks.

'No Remorse' kicks off with a mid-tempo riff and a Hammett solo before settling into quite a jagged chord pattern for the meat of the song. The closing minutes of the track ramp-up the velocity significantly with more evidence of Hetfield's almost chilling rhythm accuracy. Perhaps the most memorable moment – and one that still holds legendary status in the live set – is 'Seek And Destroy'. The dual guitar intro accented by Burton's burbling bass- line quickly settles into a mid-tempo riff packing a satisfyingly crunchy wallop. The subject matter is again fairly throwaway stuff, but the simple chorus is stunningly infectious. 'Metal Militia' finishes *Kill 'Em All* off perfectly with another slab of unadulterated thrash – moving from a straight-up scratchy riff to a more stop-start pattern, and one of Hetfield's best vocal performances on the record.

With the album recorded and being pressed to appear on the Zazula's new label Megaforce, Metallica were quickly out on the road again with another British power metal band called Raven, with whom Zazula had already forged links. The jaunt entitled the *Kill 'Em All For One* tour (Raven's new album was called *All For One*), was to kick off on the East Coast before taking in various parts of middle America en-route to a tour ending finale back in their home state of California in early September.

This was to be the band's first full tour of any great duration, and in an interview with Metal Mike of *Aardschok*, Hetfield admitted that it was a struggle at times: "There were really horrible smells on that bus as there was a lot of drinking, puking and fucking going on. You would have to get drunk to actually fall asleep on that thing as it was so horrible ... halfway through Texas the air-conditioning system broke, and it was like travelling in an oven. You woke up in the morning and your tongue was stuck to your palate, because it was 200 degrees in there!"

Heat wasn't the only issue on the trip either, as the Raven trek had the reputation for being one of the most debauched metal tours ever. The fact that the two bands were living literally on top of one another in a bus that Zazula had laid on, combined with furious levels of alcohol consumption, stoked up a truly incendiary combination.

Despite riotous off-stage behaviour, the tour went down extremely well and Metallica grew considerably as a band. The same could not always be said for Raven however, who sometimes struggled to appeal to Metallica's audience.

David Ellefson, who would become the bass player in the band Megadeth – the thrash outfit Dave Mustaine would form after his departure from Metallica – remembers running into James outside an LA venue late on that Raven tour: "I had no history with James at that time, and had recently relocated from the Mid-West myself. I really liked their music and their band though."

Ellefson had only recently met Dave Mustaine and joined his band, so he clearly felt he was in a strange position with the Metallica guys. "My involvement with James was mostly on a peer-to-peer, musician-to-musician type level, and I sometimes wondered whether I should be in opposition to them."

Ellefson, one of rock's most intelligent commentators, goes on to describe an interesting if predictable contradiction that Hetfield presented in those days. "For a guy who had such a huge presence on-stage and roars like a lion when he's singing, when he's off the stage I found him to be very introverted, and not someone who was overly animated at all. I actually admired that quality in him." Ellefson merely confirms a lot of what is known about the Hetfield persona, and in a lot of ways he completely understands it. "I get it. Obviously his stage persona is genuine. You *can* be one guy off the stage, but when you put your guitar on and saddle-up, it's almost like you're walking out of a telephone booth in *Superman* – this other guy appears."

From a musical perspective, Ellefson also recognised what was happening in the metal scene when he saw Metallica live with Raven at The Country Club in LA. "They basically played songs as I knew them on the record, and I thought they were fantastic. You could definitely tell this was a movement." What also struck Ellefson was that Hetfield, despite being the focal person in the band, obviously wasn't always comfortable with a role that involved talking to the audience between songs. Ellefson explains: "He just shut up and played, which I thought was kind of cool. He didn't try and get a reaction, he let his music get the reaction, and I admired that."

Bob Nalbandian was also at that show, and he too was impressed by how they'd improved. "That show was the first time I'd seen them with Kirk in the band and they fucking just blew me away. It wasn't just Kirk – because I actually preferred Dave Mustaine – it was just James's professionalism that was most amazing. He'd also become so much more confident."

The debut album was actually released while the band were out on that Raven tour and consequently sales were frenetic; by the end of 1983 *Kill 'Em All* had shifted an impressive 17,000 copies in the United States alone. However, in order to truly capitalise on a more general interest in the band, Zazula teamed up with a guy called Martin Hooker in the UK who had a vague knowledge of the band having heard the *No Life 'Til Leather* demo sometime earlier.

Crucially, Hooker had just founded his own record company in 1982 called Music For Nations; consequently he was on the lookout for new opportunities when a copy of *Kill 'Em All* landed on his desk, and it just happened to tick all the right boxes. Zazula and Hooker immediately bonded, and as a result, a three-album contract was set up which gave responsibility to Music For Nations for Metallica's releases in the UK and Europe as a whole.

Getting Metallica across to the UK and European audience was initially quite a challenge, particularly as the UK only received 1300 copies of the album at the outset. However, following a successful club tour, the live Metallica experience really pricked the ears of the metal public, and album sales escalated rapidly thereafter. Zazula remembers with amusement the reaction of some of the A&R people he took the album to at that time: "Most of them didn't have a clue what was going on."

By late 1983, the band were back in San Francisco enjoying the perks that their new-found fame afforded – which generally involved partying and drinking furiously with anyone who'd join them. One band that was more than willing to get involved was Armored Saint from LA who had been signed to Brian Slagel's Metal Blade label, with whom the band played a live show in November of 1983.

Apparently, vast drinking sessions ensued, culminating in Hetfield throwing beer bottles and other items out of a hotel room window into the swimming pool below. A trip to retrieve a leather jacket resulted in elevator doors being opened by Hetfield between floors, followed by a period soaking guests with a fire extinguisher he'd earlier hauled off the wall. The live shows (which included a few with Zazula's new Megaforce recruits Anthrax) didn't however suffer as a result – and if anything the band continued to grow as a unit with Hetfield himself gradually coming out of his shell as a frontman too.

Although *Kill 'Em All* had only been out a matter of months, Metallica, or more specifically Hetfield, was already giving considerable thought to writing new material. In fact the last gigs the band would undertake that year actually saw the airing of one or two new tracks that would appear on the band's next album. Even at that time, audiences who heard the new songs were surprised by the step-forward in song-writing terms which the band had already taken. The new material was ultimately destined to change *everything*.

Chapter 6

1984 and Beyond ...

When 1984 eventually did roll around, it was considerably less Orwellian than some had predicted. Far from being a time of media censorship and cultural repression, this was a rich seam of aural productivity, and it was a genuinely exciting time to be a metal-head. In many ways, 1984 was a pivotal year in this genre of music, with some of the era's more established names enjoying career high success, while new acts – of whom Metallica were one – were trying to gate-crash the party.

Iron Maiden, without doubt the most successful act to hail from the NWOBHM that Lars loved so much, would release their mighty Egyptian-themed *Powerslave* album that year, while Judas Priest – that other titan of British metal – were flying high with the accomplished *Defenders Of The Faith*. Both would continue to tour on a huge scale and release quality material for another twenty five years plus, but this would be one of several peaks for both bands, particularly Iron Maiden, whose vast stage sets and ambitious visual production set the standard for any rock band to follow. On a smaller but no less significant level, Swiss band Celtic Frost – who would influence a slew of black and death metal bands with their off-kilter and somewhat avant-garde debut entitled *Morbid Tales* – was another young act trying to access a market of largely commercial material with a much darker and extreme sound.

So, with a growing band of more like-minded followers appearing in Europe, if ever there was an opportunity for a band like Metallica to establish themselves at the forefront of a transient metal scene, 1984 was surely it.

The year did not begin exactly as planned however, because after a gig at the Channel Club in Boston on January 14,

Metallica's gear was stolen from a van outside the venue. Hetfield felt the loss of equipment more than most apparently, as he'd become particularly reliant on a particular Marshall amplifier to create exactly the guitar sound he wanted at the time. Loaned equipment from fellow Zazula-managed Anthrax was an effective contingency, and allowed them to finish that tour after which new gear could be acquired.

There was to be no let-up whatsoever though despite losing equipment, the Zazulas had cleverly mined their new relationship with Venom further by booking Metallica to tour Europe accompanying them on what would be called the *Seven Dates Of Hell* tour. Dave Marrs, whose involvement with Hetfield dated back to school days in Downey, was still working for the band as Lars's drum roadie, and remembers this Venom tour being a turning point for him. "We listened to Mercyful Fate pretty much 24/7 on that tour on the bus as I recall, and then when we were in Denmark and we went to Sweet Silence Studios, the band were actually there. At that point they didn't have enough money to keep me in Europe so I had to come home. I don't really feel any regrets though as I didn't really know what the hell I was doing up there. When you go out on the road you find out real quick whether it's meant for you or not, and it just wasn't meant for me."

So, another of the important figures in Hetfield's early life leaves the story, and like Hugh Tanner before him, life in a metal band just wasn't the career path that was right for Dave. Marrs, like Tanner and McGovney, was a key link back to the early days in Downey, and his departure left Hetfield on his own to plough a lone furrow with his band.

Just as they had on the US tour with Venom the previous year, Metallica went – as Venom guitarist Jeff Dunn bluntly described it when talking to writer Joel McIver – "fuckin' nuts on the first night." The two bands clearly had some serious chemistry going on, and that overflowed into a lot of debauched drinking chaos that continued until the tour finale at the Aardschok Festival in Holland on February 12.

In the festival crowd that day was German metal fan Mille Petrozza, who himself would go on to form an uncompromising thrash band of his own called Kreator. They would become one of Europe's premier thrash flag-bearers during the 1980s, and would utterly refuse to change their style in the lean days of the 1990s, a time when thrash was driven largely underground.

Petrozza remembers being inspired by Hetfield and Metallica even before that Aardschok appearance: "When *Kill 'Em All* came out, it was like some kind of sonic revolution. There were bands out there like Venom and Accept that played fast, but Metallica took this style to a level of perfection." When discussing that day in Zwolle, Holland, Petrozza is equally reverential: "We were excited when we heard that they would open for Venom and everyone went there to see Metallica. It was an experience I'll never forget."

Venom's Jeff Dunn acknowledged the success of the tour when he spoke to writer Joel McIver, and also remembered the specifics of how the bands interacted. "Lars was always the spokesperson and always had the most to say. James was always down-to-earth, just a genuinely nice guy who seemed to be pleased to be there and was there for the love of it."

While that tour roared on, the band, Hooker and his label Music For Nations began giving serious thought to the second Metallica album so much so that they chose to release 'Jump In The Fire' – that 'filler' track from *Kill 'Em All* – as a single, along with live versions of 'Seek And Destroy' and 'Phantom Lord'. It was essentially just a stop-gap release, but it served to sustain fans' attention until new material was ready.

Instead of returning to America to record however, the band instead chose to remain in Europe – in Lars's home country Denmark to be precise. The unenviable responsibility of following up *Kill 'Em All* from behind the mixing desk would go to the calm Danish producer Flemming Rasmussen, whose Sweet Silence Studios would become the band's home for the next few weeks.

Rasmussen was an easy-going guy who'd come to the band's attention on the back of British traditional rock band Rainbow's *Difficult To Cure* record, to which he'd given a really energetic gloss back in 1981. Given that he'd dealt with the mix of egos and personalities that Rainbow collectively involved, he was the ideal choice on both a human and sonic level.

What the band definitely did not want was a repeat of the *Kill*

'Em All sessions, where they felt they could have had more help from their producer. What they really needed was someone who could refine, or even better, develop the band's sound, and with Rasmussen they felt they had the right man. Not just that, the fact that this was Lars's hometown was significant too, and in a lot of ways that location had the effect of being something of a safety blanket for the band. Because it had taken all the available funds at the time to even get the band into the studio, they were going to make full use of those facilities by sleeping there too. In any case, they certainly couldn't have afforded hotel rooms at the time, even if they'd wanted them.

Consequently, when that Venom tour ended, the band drove to Copenhagen in February, as Dave Marrs mentioned, and began living and rehearsing at Sweet Silence which, as Marrs also mentioned, had recently been used by Mercyful Fate and their charismatic singer King Diamond. Metallica album number two would be called *Ride The Lightning*, and the road to making it happen began and ended at Sweet Silence.

Rasmussen remembers his first involvement with Hetfield. "The first time I met him was in the studio, and he's got a pretty strong mind about what he wants from a sound perspective." There was an immediate problem with that however, given that Hetfield's favourite guitar amp had disappeared at that Boston show with Anthrax. Hetfield and Rasmussen had to bang heads a little to arrive at a solution, as Flemming remembers: "We started out playing some *Kill 'Em All* tracks so I could hear what he was talking about, and we started testing guitar amps which took a couple of days."

The issue with the stolen amp was that it had been modified which meant, as Rasmussen bluntly states: "Nobody remembered what the fuck had gone on so we were all kind of lost. What we ended up with was something very different, which from my point of view was brilliant because I could then work on the getting the sounds I wanted."

It seems that even at this early career stage, Hetfield had developed something of a unique guitar sound, and it needed the Danish cool of Rasmussen to make best of use of James's newly found need to sound like nobody else on the planet, as Flemming explains, "He liked the fact that he had his own sound and wasn't trying to copy someone else's. I think we took most of the recording process to pretty much get his thing. So we ended up looking for something that was new but also sounded something like his own stolen amp." But what did the Dane make of the man on a personal level? "I always considered James to be an angry young man. He had a great attitude I thought though."

It does seem that a cool and knowledgeable figure like Rasmussen was the perfect foil for the opinionated Hetfield back in 1984. By tempering Hetfield's inner angst and channelling those feelings down a purely creative route, it might just be that the *Ride The Lightning* sessions under Rasmussen's care were the embryonic beginnings of a more musically mature James Hetfield.

While the recording process rolled on (it would be split into two chunks: February/March and part of June), the business acumen of Hetfield was being put under close scrutiny even at this early stage, as Rasmussen noticed: "They were negotiating a new deal because they were on that independent [Megaforce] label. They had different conversations with various labels and he was a big part of that. He's a smart guy."

Also during that break between the two recording periods at Sweet Silence, the band headed to London to play two shows at the renowned Marquee Club, which successfully kept the pot boiling for a UK audience who were now well aware that a new Metallica record was relatively imminent.

Originally, Metallica were meant to be touring Europe with two other Megaforce acts, The Rods and Canadian thrashers Exciter, but the 'Hell On Earth' tour as it was billed had to be scrapped – rumoured to be due to poor ticket sales. Dan Beehler, the drummer and vocalist with Exciter recalls an encounter with James in London around that time. "Music For Nations rented two apartments in Baker Street; Metallica were in the basement and we were above," Beehler remembers. "I would go down and hang out with James and the boys, and we'd party large."

Amusingly, Exciter's business wasn't done in London on that trip either, and they ended up in some unusual parts of town, as Dan recounts: "We ended up playing Walthamstow, and the Metallica guys were there!" Beehler also remembers being somewhat surprised by Hetfield's stature: "When I first saw the back of the *Kill 'Em All* album cover, I thought he was a little guy. Then when I met him he was pretty tall. He's a super guy and was totally happy-go-lucky, and loved to have a good time back then."

Thereafter, Metallica returned to Copenhagen, put the album to bed as it were, and went out on a brief four-stop tour with New York grease-paint rockers Twisted Sister, finishing on June 10.

Seventeen days later, on June 27, 1984, *Ride The Lightning* eventually landed, and with an almighty thud too. Zazula had managed to release it on his own Megaforce label in the US, had Music For Nations do the honours in the UK, and had negotiated a way to get another label called Roadrunner to handle it in Holland.

The response across the board was one of open-mouthed disbelief. Sure, *Kill 'Em All* was an aggressive, heavy affair and a fabulous debut but *this* ...? 'This' was something very different indeed. The leap forward in both sound and song-writing from *Kill 'Em All* was so marked, one could be forgiven for questioning if this was even the same band. Hetfield's contribution particularly had morphed from being in retrospect quite an awkward debut, into a far more domineering role both vocally, and in terms of his increasingly stellar rhythm guitar precision.

One of the most impressive features however was Rasmussen's production, which while massively capturing the heaviness of the band's sound, had found a way of giving that sound space to breathe – with devastating effect. When asked in 1988 about the way *Ride The Lightning* sounded, Hetfield bluntly stated, "Flemming was in a reverb daze." True, the album did have a lot of reverb, but nobody could question the songs in any way.

Even the front cover, which depicted an electric chair somehow suspended in what looks like a night sky beneath that now familiar logo, was a more mature statement of the band's rapid growth, and all this before a needle was even dropped on track one.

As opening tracks go, it wouldn't be overstating things to say that 'Fight Fire With Fire' is one of Metallica's most telling compositions ever. Note the word 'composition' too, because one of *Ride The Lightning*'s most impressive features generally is its implacable will to create complex yet powerful songs, where previous material had been delivered much more crudely by comparison.

Starting with a delicate but highly ominous acoustic intro, the track festers into a terrifying fade-in that in turn heralds a riff of warp-speed brutality. Hetfield's insanely accurate picking should really carry a 'Don't try this at home' message before Ulrich and Burton pile in shortly ahead of a very different Hetfield vocal delivery. The *Kill 'Em All* version of James Hetfield's scream lacked tonal variety at times, whereas now his tone was of snarled and almost military urgency – completely in keeping with a song about nuclear Armageddon.

To this day it's a stunning lesson in measured aggression, and a moment Metallica would do well to better in their entire career. The song signs off with the sound of a nuclear explosion that leads directly into the title track, with no discernable pause for breath. Its whining dual guitar intro settles into a mid-tempo chug with Hetfield taking on the role of a condemned man awaiting his electric chair fate. It's again far more complex, taking in a progressive mid-section and a stirring Hammett guitar solo, before returning exactly to where it began.

The colossal 'For Whom The Bell Tolls' is next, beginning with – strangely enough – the toll of a bell. Burton's distorted bass harmony joins in along with a ploddingly mesmeric riff whose desire to be in no hurry whatsoever is actually a blessing. Rumoured to be inspired by Hemmingway's novel of the same name which tackles the plight of soldiers in the Spanish Civil war, it's another incredible vocal exercise from Hetfield, and a regular in the band's live set ever since.

The album's biggest surprise comes next in the form of the achingly angst-ridden 'Fade To Black', which in one fell swoop launched the Metallica sound into a completely new dimension. Its delicate acoustic beginning combines with Hetfield's equally delicate (for him at least) singing, reflecting on concepts of hopelessness and suicide. It builds steadily via a choppy mid-section to a faster crescendo, and it would be the first of several more melodic, heavy songs over the next few years.

'Trapped Under Ice' is next and it's a return to pure speed after the initial twitchy riff slides seamlessly into a full-on thrash classic.

There is a mid song-breakdown, with a brief sing and response arrangement prior to a rapid Hammett solo, and a return to the original verse – killer stuff. 'Escape' is a complete anomaly if truth be told. It's a mid-tempo chugger with no real lyrical depth, which builds in a sing-a-long chorus more favoured by the kinds of hair metal bands that Metallica left LA to avoid. On the plus side there's a tasty Hammett solo before the wail of a siren signals this unusual song's conclusion.

For many though, the focal point of *Ride The Lightning* is the penultimate track, the unforgettable 'Creeping Death' – it would be tough to disagree. Kicking in with a monstrous, repeated guitar salvo, it eases into a fluidly effective riff, driving Hetfield's Biblical tale referencing *The Tale of The Firstborn* from the book of Exodus. It's complex too, with a chilling Phrygian chord mid-song section that quickly became a popular part of the live performance. It encompasses everything that the band was about at the time and not surprisingly, it is the most played live song in the band's career.

The album closes with an instrumental entitled 'The Call Of Ktulu', an epic feast of metal thought to be inspired by the H.P Lovecraft short story called 'The Call Of Cthulhu'. Whether it's actually inspired by that or something else less sinister, as the hilariously misprinted 'The Cat Of Ktulu' (as it was on some versions) may suggest, is irrelevant: it's a mighty fine way to finish a colossal album.

While all the excitement of the album release was raging, there was a management issue to resolve, as well as a tour to embark on. It had become obvious that Metallica's relationship with the enthusiastic and extremely generous Zazula partnership and their Megaforce label was probably running out of time. While there is little doubting the fact that without them the band may have struggled to ever release an album at all, it had come to the point where they'd actually outgrown Megaforce and therefore needed the support of a big label to make good on the huge potential that *Ride The Lightning* suggested was possible.

Admirably, Zazula concurs with that theory too: "It was really in the band's best interest to move on. In those days it actually meant something to be on a record label." The switchover to a major league record label was therefore in the pipeline, and a New Yorker called Michael Alago had already taken small steps to make it happen, as he himself explains: "I had started working for the Elektra label in March of 1983 and my job was to sign and develop new artists."

As it happened, Zazula and Alago's paths had already crossed given that the band Raven were signed to Megaforce and Alago had been involved with recording demos for them. Receiving a copy of *Kill 'Em All* changed everything for Alago however. "It slayed me. So one day I flew to San Francisco to see the band and they just fucking blew me away. I knew right then that these people were extraordinary."

Although the outgoing Alago spoke to Ulrich in San Francisco that night, and made the band aware of who he was and what he did, he would have to wait until the summer of 1984 to take it any further. But Alago was definitely immediately impressed by what he saw in Hetfield too, even after only one meeting. "I saw James as a natural born leader and a real wild child as a performer. He was one of the best even in those early days."

As it turned out, Zazula and Megaforce had laid on a showcase gig for their acts on August 3, at the Roseland in New York consisting of Metallica, Anthrax and Raven, and it would prove a memorable night for several reasons, not least because several observers suggest Metallica put their label-mates to the sword. Alago remembers it vividly: "That night belonged to Metallica and the energy in the air was electric. They performed brilliantly and I was just so amped by what I saw."

Alago wasn't the only industry heavy there that night as it turned out. Also impressed by the Metallica experience was Cliff Burnstein, the co-founder of an artist management company called Q Prime. Burnstein and his Q Prime company would soon become a significant part of Metallica's world, and Alago was keen that the band immediately became a part of his too. "I ran backstage that night and practically barricaded the door shut, while I told them how much I loved them and wanted them in my personal and business world."

Whatever Alago managed to impart that night while locked in Metallica's dressing room at the Roseland must have worked. "The next day they came by the Elektra offices and we got some

Chinese food and some beers, and the rest is history. You better believe it!" he admits with some considerable pride.

So within a couple of days, Metallica signed contracts with Q Prime to manage them, and then with Elektra as their label (the Zazula's Megaforce label went on to sell over 37 million albums in later years, working with seminal thrash acts such as Anthrax, Testament and Overkill, and that shrewd and visionary couple have justifiably become revered as major players in the history of metal). Although the Elektra deal was not necessarily the best available in financial terms, the band recognised the label's reputation for allowing their artists a certain level of creative license. Not just that, heavy metal – or more specifically thrash metal – was a hot commodity in 1984. Therefore, it was important to find a label that was at least half-way receptive to that.

As part of an interview with *Thrasher* magazine, Hetfield himself commented on the trend: "Right then there were bands being signed, snatched up on major labels. All the major labels were saying, 'Oh, metal's like this new thing, get in on the money right now.'" Although the band received some criticism for selling-out to a big label, it didn't bother them at all, and would merely be the start of many future accusations of commercialism that they'd have to deal with.

Elektra began as they meant to continue – the label actually re-issued the most recent album soon after taking the band on, and accompanied the identical release with a lavish EP that appeared as a 12" single. The focal point of the single was the stunning 'Creeping Death', whereas the B-side would include two cover versions of Diamond Head tracks 'Blitzkrieg' and 'Am I Evil?'. Both versions turned out incredibly well, and would regularly be aired as part of the live set.

With new impetus provided by the re-issue and the EP, *Ride The Lightning* really started to catch-on, and all that despite virtually zero radio play. To capitalise further, the band would obviously tour extensively, first of all through Europe beginning in November, and then through the States after a festive break in San Francisco.

During that break, Metallica's flatmates in London, Exciter, were due to play a show in Berkeley, but as Dan Beehler explains, things didn't go to plan: "We cancelled the gig because the lights didn't show up, and I'll never forget James standing in the street saying 'Hey man, you gotta play, man!', and we said, 'No, we're leaving', to which James replied, 'Nobody else gives a shit. Why don't you guys just play the fuckin' gig?'"

Dan finds Hetfield's reaction amusing even now. "I remember him standing there beside our van in the street. He's looking at me shaking his head saying, 'We play with no lights, why the fuck can't you?'"

Once the American leg of the tour kicked off, Metallica co-headlined with shock rockers WASP for the first half, before headlining the second part on their own with Armored Saint as support. Anyone who witnessed that tour, which was amusingly called 'Bang The Head That Doesn't Bang', was stunned at how far the band had come since it had last been out on the road.

When that tour rolled through Texas, James would meet another aspiring group of musicians who were trying to carve out their own part of metal immortality. That band was called Pantera, and their bass player Rex Brown recalls hooking up. "We had seen them on the Raven tour in a tiny place and nobody was there, but we never got to meet them."

Pantera were at that time a glam-influenced band of a distinctly Southern flavour, with their ace card being the inhuman guitar skills of one Darrel 'Dimebag' Abbott. "We were playing clubs in the South West at that time, and Philip [Anselmo] wasn't even in our band by this time. Anyhow, Dime and me go on-stage with James and the guys and we go through several songs from their first record."

Even at that time, Hetfield had a considerable aura of respect according to Rex. "We looked up to him so much, we just kind of let him talk. He ... definitely had a mystique. He had something going on upstairs, but you didn't really know what the fuck it was." A friendship was cemented, and the careers of Pantera and Metallica would have considerable interplay over the next fifteen years.

David Ellefson was somebody else who caught that tour, and he really noticed the change, particularly in Hetfield: "They came through and played the Palladium in Hollywood on the *Ride The Lightning* Tour, and holy smokes they were ferocious." It wasn't just

THE WOLF AT METALLICA'S DOOR

how they sounded that Ellefson remembers either. "It's impregnated on my mind watching James come out. He had his shirt off, looked great, and was just ferocious. He came out roaring with confidence and was like a lion up there. He commanded the entire room. I was just floored at how great he'd become."

Another character that would gradually ooze into Metallica's world was a young guy from Arizona called Eric Braverman. Nowadays he describes himself as a 'natural history consultant'. Braverman is one of life's characters, with a burning enthusiasm for everything that impacts on his world. Those things would vary from wild outdoor pursuits, to Slayer, and to filmmaking, but back in 1986 he was a young metal-head in Tucson trying to make his way in metal journalism with his friend Joe Lopez.

Braverman remembers meeting James and Cliff one night on that tour. "We went down – and in those days you could just call a publicist, and they'd set you up instead of going through all kinds of crazy shit – and saw the band on that tour. I met them after that show and had a smoke with Cliff Burton; the only one who wanted a smoke." Braverman would operate on the fringes of the band thereafter, initially as a fan, but he would later have a vital role to play.

Established friend Brian Slagel also saw a lot of James on that tour, and increasingly hung out with him after shows. He definitely noticed a difference in Hetfield's level of on-stage proficiency, but saw little change in James on a personal level." We'd go out after a show and hang out quite a lot actually, but for me they hadn't changed at all. Especially James."

When the tour ended, Metallica had successfully rammed their music down the throats of a vast spread of the American metal-buying public, and while undoubtedly an exhausting experience, it was a huge commercial success. Understandably, the band needed some time off, so part of 1985 was spent back in San Francisco relaxing, with maybe half an eye on ideas for their next album for which recording was scheduled to begin in September.

Katon de Pena's band Hirax were touring San Francisco while Metallica were off the road, so James decided to go out and see their show. "I remember Metallica was getting really popular and people were starting to get jealous of them," Katon remembers.

"James and I were outside a club and were walking to a liquor store when this metal dude yells at him: 'Hey, Metallica suck!' I'll never forget the cool way James handled this dick. He didn't get mad, he just turned round and said two words: 'Your mother!' This guy had no answer because James had made him look completely stupid with just two words. I really admired that."

Before the next album recording sessions started though, Metallica travelled to Europe for an appearance at the famous Monsters of Rock festival at Castle Donington. An awful piece of scheduling resulted in Metallica appearing sandwiched between hair metal bands Bon Jovi and Ratt, and James famously announced to the 70,000 strong Donington crowd as his band wandered on-stage: "If you came here to see spandex, eye make-up, and the words 'Oh baby' in every fuckin' song, this ain't the fuckin' band!"

As if that huge crowd wasn't enough, Metallica appeared at Oakland's Day On The Green festival a couple of weeks later at a show that would be one of their career live highlights, in front of a staggering 90,000 screaming metal-heads. Hetfield's friend Fred Cotton was one of those 90,000 and Hetfield's performance that day left a mark on him. "It was incredible man, with that hometown crowd, and they just fucking blew the whole place away. I would have hated to have to set up and play after them that day."

Not only did they 'blow the place away', Hetfield also got in hot water for trashing the dressing room as he told *Playboy* some years later: "A buddy and I, completely ripped on Jagermeister, got it into our heads that the deli tray and the fruit had to go through a little vent. 'The vent is not big enough. Let's make a hole!' The trailer was ruined. Bill Graham – RIP – was the promoter. I was summoned to his office."

This kind of behaviour did not always go down well and Hetfield at least considered changing his ways: "I realised at that point that there was more to being in a band than pissing people off and smashing things up."

This was to be the end of a hugely productive chapter in the band's early history, and with only one more live appearance at the Lorely Metal Hammer Fest in Germany on September 14 before

Metallica re-entered the studio, it was also a period that offered no respite from hard work. Fortunately, both individually and collectively, they were up to that challenge, and Ulrich had already begun the laborious task of tracking drums for what would be the new record.

Chapter 7

The Master

Although by the autumn of 1985 Metallica were certainly making large waves in their world, it's important to stress that even at this stage their impact on the global mainstream music market was still relatively insignificant. Music is obviously about much more than heavy metal, so to hope that a metal band, and an extreme one at that, was about to gatecrash the upper reaches of the *Billboard* charts alongside the Whitney Houstons of this world, was a forlorn one in the cautiously conservative days of the mid-1980s.

This thrash metal thing was very much a movement within a movement, and it would be some years before a band like Metallica would leak like a vile gas into the living rooms of 'regular' people. Any such infiltration – by supposedly heavier bands at least – was far more likely to be achieved by an Ozzy Osborne, a Bon Jovi or a Van Halen, all of whom were working on big albums for a 1986 release, and who more importantly presented an image and a sound which was much easier for the public to stomach. That said, there was still important Metallica business to be done and this was now a band who took their music commitments unbelievably seriously, and with a focus on detail bordering on the compulsive.

Before they could completely immerse themselves in the depths of studio creativity, Metallica first had to decide where their third album would be recorded. Contrary to popular opinion, Metallica had – at least in principle – initially considered other options other than *Ride The Lightning*'s producer Flemming Rasmussen. It was even rumoured that Martin Birch, producer of some of Iron Maiden's best albums, was mentioned in that process, and you could only imagine that an idea like that had Ulrich's head spinning round like a scene from *The Exorcist*, given his partiality for all things NWOBHM.

Nobody was arguing with the first-class job Rasmussen had done with the last record – particularly given his rapidly closing time window – but there was a feeling that Hetfield wanted the new material to be recorded in the US, and Rasmussen wasn't totally thrilled about travelling over there to do it. What settled the issue in the end was Ulrich's urge to again work in Copenhagen, which made the choice of Rasmussen even more appealing.

The band arrived at Sweet Silence in September of 1985, after Hetfield and Ulrich had spent time earlier that year working on ideas for the new album. Unlike the *Ride The Lightning* sessions where the band had crashed in the studio and in friends of Lars's apartments, this time the band's finances stretched to hotel accommodation close to Sweet Silence. Not that they used it much, as Rasmussen remembers: "We worked nights generally; starting at 8pm and working through until the morning. Then the band would go back to their hotel, pig out on the breakfast buffet and go to bed."

Nonetheless, the hotel accommodation was entirely necessary. In contrast to their two previous studio stints – which had lasted two weeks and one month respectively – the three full torturous months it took to record the third album was totally unprecedented. The reason for that stems back to the single-minded perfectionism that Hetfield and Ulrich had honed as their career had gathered steam.

Not only did they now record with a manic attention to detail, they also extended that discipline further down the line, and applied it equally to the potentially laborious disciplines of mixing and mastering. That wasn't all either, because the songs that they were working on for this record took the complexities of earlier work to a completely new level, which only served to stretch every part of the album-making process out even further. They did at least initiate the sessions superbly by arriving fully prepared, as Rasmussen acknowledges with some relief: "The songs were almost all arranged when they came to the studio; as they have always been renowned for doing really good demos, and that was the case this time too." Although the album would be mixed back in the states at Amigo studios in North Hollywood by Michael

Wagener, the bulk of the recording work was done in these three months in Denmark.

Rasmussen recognised the change in Hetfield immediately the sessions began. "When we came into the studio this time he'd improved significantly. He'd gained a lot of experience from being on the road, and as a guitar player he'd become fast and extremely accurate. When we did *Ride The Lightning* I thought he was one of the best guitar players I'd ever worked with. Now he was light-years ahead of anything I'd ever heard before."

Flemming thought that Hetfield had grown up considerably as a person, and in a short space of time too. "James is one of the most stand-up guys ever. There are tons of layers below the persona he projects, but he makes a pretty good job of hiding that – at least he certainly did in those days. It's probably part of the process of growing up that you realise you don't have to be embarrassed about emotions and stuff."

That appraisal of the mature Hetfield psyche in 1985 would prove to be prophetically astute, and his opinion as to how much he'd developed as a guitar player would become increasingly evident as these third album sessions progressed. Hetfield was slowly evolving as a musician and a man, and the evidence would be deeply ingrained in the new album, which would be entitled *Master Of Puppets*.

Mention that name to any metal fan, and you're likely to be waiting most of the day for the stream of positive expletives to come to an end. Ask a few non-metal types if they've heard of it and you might just get the odd nod of vague recognition. *Master Of Puppets*, despite its rightful place alongside Slayer's astonishing *Reign In Blood* as one of the two best thrash metal albums of all-time, is still just a thrash metal album. A phenomenal record, but one that nonetheless – and despite its untouchable reputation – really didn't cross over into the genuine mainstream.

What it did do however was herald the dawning of a new type of powerful metal: metal with crushing brutality as expected by extreme fans, but also with texture, complexity and huge lyrical depth that would quickly attract a slew of new listeners. It's truly a one-off, and for many it was the finest hour of Hetfield and Co (although it wouldn't come even close to later output in terms of sheer butts-on-seats sales).

Before we look at the specifics, and the huge role that Hetfield contributed to them, the general sound of the album is something that's definitely worth closer examination. Despite being recorded in the same studio as *Ride The Lightning*, the two albums sound nothing like each other. The former had an aura of airy approachability, whereas the latter sounded distant and a little claustrophobic – a feel that perfectly suited the song's repressive subject matter. According to Rasmussen, everyone had become a lot more dedicated to making a great sounding record this time around. "On *Ride The Lightning* we'd been meticulous as to how we did things. This time it was bordering on the obsessional. I think we all, including me, felt that we had an epic album. James and I were very keen to thicken everything up considerably on *Master Of Puppets*. Up until then he didn't have much experience of guitar dubbing effects and we used way more of those this time. The resulting overall sound was consequently much bigger, and those multi-layered guitar tracks Rasmussen mentioned definitely gave the songs an incredibly meaty facia.

It wasn't just Hetfield's guitar parts that underwent overhaul either. Where Ulrich's drum sound on *Ride The Lightning* was subject to quite a lot of reverb, giving it a rather relaxed feel, here it was as if every atom of air had been sucked from the studio when he laid down his drum tracks – it really is that dry and direct.

Combine that with a level of song-writing complexity (three tracks would exceed the eight-minute mark) that was a further step ahead of anything they'd embarked on previously, and you had the kind of album whose sound and composition would simply refuse to date. It has to be said though that while *Master Of Puppets* was a significant forward step for the band, it was not as big a progression as had occurred from *Kill 'Em All* to *Ride The Lightning*.

As a spotty teenager at an oppressive Scottish boarding school, I recall breaking every school rule imaginable to go into our local town to buy a cassette copy of *Master Of Puppets*. I was part of a select group of metal fans, although in all truth Van Halen, Ozzy

Osborne or Iron Maiden was as heavy as we dared go at that time.

There was something about the *Kerrang!* review of the new Metallica album though which prompted this daring step into the unknown, and when the opening classical chords introducing 'Battery' chimed out, we knew we'd made a choice that would change our musical taste for life. First of all it's played on a traditional, almost Spanish-sounding acoustic guitar, which should offer some kind of comfort. It doesn't. Then, in a manner so measured but so terrifyingly powerful, that lilting acoustic part is repeated, but this time by a salvo that sounds like a thousand guitars (given Hetfield's fondness for tracking, it may well have been). Rasmussen delivers the facts however: "It was eight rhythm guitar tracks on there."

Truly, it's a stunning moment, and one that Hetfield and his buddies would never ever match for sheer dramatic effect. What follows is a pulverising riff from the rhythm lord Hetfield himself, whose direction and form is actually quite difficult to pin-down. Then Hetfield's vocals arrive, and immediately they're deeper, more mature and generally far more menacing than at any time previously. Gone are the screams, the occasional off-key notes and the weird pronunciation.

Instead, we get precise, insistent and controlled delivery from a man who clearly knows what he is doing, and it's still just the first track. Not content with that, Hetfield also dials in a sublimely appropriate lead break that merely served to complete his command of all he surveyed, and that lead prowess would be one that we'd see much more of in years to come.

The title track which follows almost without pause is a vast, twisting serpent of a thing, and a stark anti-drugs warning at that. As compositions go, it's as complex and well-crafted as the band had ever attempted, and the melancholy mid-section offsets the power of the main verse and chorus superbly. It's a thoughtful and cautionary Hetfield lyric too.

Track three is perhaps the runt of the litter. Entitled 'The Thing That Should Not Be', it's a plodding tale of some kind of mythical creature maybe, and while being undeniably very heavy, it's by far the least arresting moment on the album.

Much more interesting, and developing on 'Fade to Black's style of quiet build-up from *Ride The Lightning*, 'Welcome Home (Sanitarium)' is another example of how far the band had come. A shimmeringly clean intro (it actually starts in mono, before Rasmussen flicks a switch over to stereo) decorated with some sublime Hammett soloing, slides into another suffocating lyric by Hetfield. Its lyrics relate the feelings of somebody incarcerated in some kind of mental institution. That person's frustration with his plight builds alongside the tempo of the track that culminates in a violently angry conclusion.

Next up is 'Disposable Heroes' which continues the album's underlying theme of control, this time dealing with the issue of front-line soldiers being sent to their death. Musically it's a masterpiece, courtesy of another incredibly precise Hetfield riff and some of his most compelling vocal work to date. A new feature on *Master of Puppets* is Hetfield's ability to actually become the character of every track (in this case an uncaring army superior urging lesser soldiers to expend their lives for a cause), and that acting ability adds so much more credibility to all the songs.

Likewise with 'Leper Messiah', where Hetfield points a finger directly at the controlling effect of organised religion. It's a bitter attack for sure, and you wonder whether his own childhood experiences were an inspiration for this hugely underrated track.

Continuing the theme they'd started previously on *Ride The Lightning, Master of Puppets* too would have an instrumental track, and in this case it's a gem simply called 'Orion'. Beginning with a crunchy, composed riff, before branching off into some clever interplay between Hetfield and Hammett, the latter part of the tune is all Burton, with a stunningly delivered bass solo thrown in too.

Finally, and entirely appropriately, the album is brought to a breathless conclusion with a pure slab of unadulterated thrash metal, entitled 'Damage Inc'. Again, fading-in with a terrifying malevolence – an effect created by Rasmussen by reversing some pre-recorded bass sounds – it's a brutal white-knuckle trip through a Hetfield lyrical composition focusing almost exclusively on an explosive release of aggression.

After the recording process finished in Denmark in December of 1985, Metallica played another live show in Sacramento again supporting Y&T and then yet another on New Year's eve with Metal Church, Exodus and Ellefson and Mustaine's band Megadeth. As a taste for what the new album offered, the band debuted 'Disposable Heroes' as well as the title track which were both received with suitable enthusiasm by a rowdy San Francisco audience at the city's Civic Centre.

In the January of 1986, *Master Of Puppets* was sent for mixing by Michael Wagener at his studios in Hollywood, while the band split up to conduct European press prior to the album's release. Wagener, a gifted producer, saw two sides to the young Hetfield at the time. "James was young and wild of course, but he still had an impressive calm when it came to understanding the direction of the album." Not just that, it also appeared that Hetfield came to Hollywood with a fixed plan as to how the record should sound, even after the three punishing months recording in Denmark. "He and Lars attended every single mixing session, and James had very definite needs. Those needs combined with my personal vision are what you hear on the album."

The cover art for the album was a compelling image too, featuring rows of white gravestones that look like a war cemetery, above which are a large pair of god-like hands seemingly influencing events from high above.

While Ulrich was roaming around his beloved Europe telling anyone who'd listen how good his record would be, Hetfield was back in the Bay Area taking things just a little easier. What that actually involved was hanging around with friends like Fred Cotton, who he hadn't seen much of lately due to his considerable Metallica commitments.

Cotton and two other buddies had ended up forming a joke band playing awful cover tunes, as he remembers: "We got ourselves on a bill at some nightclub, and our aim was to be as shitty as possible. We wanted to see how long it was before they kicked us off-stage." That band would become known as Spastik Children, and it was a matter of time before Hetfield got involved with his friend's fun act, as Cotton confirms: "We'd already played once by the time James came back from recording, and I told him all about it and he said, 'Fuck, I wanna play drums.'"

According to Cotton, the point was not the music, it was about being shitty, and Hetfield apparently relished his temporary role as the band's drummer. From all reliable reports he could play a bit too, as Cotton testifies: "Oh yeah, he was a pounder. He liked to smash on the right cymbal ... it was all about just having a lot of fun."

Cotton was undoubtedly a valuable friend in those days in 1986, and it certainly appears that that interaction was good for James, and even served as a calming reality check away from the serious business of Metallica. "We were like fuckin' brothers back then. I taught him to ride a motorcycle and we used to skateboard together too." Cotton also remembers with fondness that, "James would always get ahead of himself though, which is how he ended up breaking things." Cotton's mention of motorcycles is significant. While James probably didn't have either the time or the financial means to pursue this interest, in later life he would rectify that situation by accruing a collection of bikes, trucks and old Chevrolet cars from the year of his birth.

When Lars returned from hawking *Master Of Puppets* round Europe, he and James took a vacation together in the resort of Nassau in the Bahamas, while their management company Q Prime looked for the best tour options for the band that summer. What they came up with was a masterstroke, as the band would be touring the US extensively with ex-Black Sabbath frontman Ozzy Osborne.

After parting ways with Sabbath in 1979, Osborne went on to achieve considerable success with his own band, greatly helped by the guitar virtuosity of Randy Rhoads. Tragically, just as things were really starting to roll for them all, Rhoads was killed when a light aircraft which was 'buzzing' the band's tour bus (on a day off in 1982) crashed and exploded into flames. The following year Osbourne recruited one time Ratt and Rough Cutt guitarist Jake E Lee to fill the late Rhoads's rather large shoes.

That line-up released the well-received *Bark At The Moon* album in 1983, and had been working on a follow-up called *The Ultimate Sin*, which would be coincidentally released the day after *Master Of Puppets* on February 22, 1986. Although the two bands were worlds apart in sound, Ozzy was certainly on a commercial high and was a significant draw, so any exposure Metallica got on such a high profile tour could only be a positive.

Following *Master Of Puppets*' release on February 21, and thanks to Lars's efforts in Europe and a thorough media campaign by Music For Nations, sales were phenomenal. This was particularly encouraging, and it seemed that thrash metal was gaining a level of respectability that was unprecedented previously. In both Europe and the US, there was now a slew of acts appearing with serious thrash pretensions, although none of them – with the possible exception of Slayer – had captured the public's attention quite like Metallica.

Slayer, while always regarded as one of the original big four thrash bands, was not in any way similar to Metallica in ideology, or in fact sound. They relied much more on an unmistakably evil menace, which although becoming gradually more refined over the years, was far less progressive, and therefore less commercially viable than that of Metallica.

Therefore with an emerging undercurrent of support at their backs, Metallica embarked on the three-month tour with Ozzy Osbourne beginning on March 27 – it would be a challenge to see if they could turn the ear of the main act's far more mainstream following. As it turned out, they needn't have worried because the gigs were a rousing success, and Metallica's harder edged riffs were simply lapped up by all who saw them. More dates were added later in the summer as well as a European tour in the autumn.

What they hadn't bargained on however was what happened on July 26 before a show at Evansville, Indiana. Hetfield, had been skateboarding before the show, and as Fred Cotton had alluded to earlier, had perhaps 'got ahead of himself' and ended up breaking his wrist. Obviously that night's show had to be cancelled, but there was a bigger problem in that Hetfield wouldn't be able to play guitar because of his plastered arm until late September. Fortunately, John Marshall – who was at that time Kirk's roadie – was drafted in to play Hetfield's rhythm parts from the wings for not only the remaining Ozzy dates, but also part of the upcoming European jaunt with old buddies Anthrax.

When asked how hard it was to dial-in Hetfield's otherworldly rhythm parts, Marshall was honest when speaking to writer Joel McIver: "Well, the hard part was trying to match the vibe and intensity of his guitar playing. I knew how to play the riffs and song arrangements okay, but getting the feel right was difficult." Marshall then revealed his real fear: "I think I was more worried about what the rest of the band thought, than what the audience thought."

In all truth it didn't matter what the band thought, because in reality they were lucky to even have a stand-in, far less one who was already in a band (Marshall was a member of Metal Church). That level of experience definitely helped Marshall deliver something close to Hetfield levels of precision. "I remember feeling really excited, a little stunned that they had actually asked me, and a little nervous," Marshall remembers.

In mid-September 1986, Metallica flew to Europe to play ten shows with Anthrax in the UK, prior to heading over to the mainland to continue the 'Damage Inc' tour on their own. That UK tour with Anthrax would turn out to be a massive turning point for thrash metal in Britain, given the frenetic audiences that greeted all of these shows.

Anthrax had their own agenda; their own *Among The Living* record was due to be released the following March, representing a career high-water mark. Anthrax drummer Charlie Benante remembers how James was on that frenetic UK tour. "At that point we were on a real good friendly basis, and after the shows we would just hang-out and talk about whatever." The two bands clearly had a lot in common from their early dealings back in the Music Building in New York, but there was a suspicion that even now they were heading in slightly different directions, and that would inevitably make hanging out a little more tricky.

After laying waste to ten theatre-size venues in the UK with Anthrax, including one particularly insane show at London's Hammersmith Odeon on September 21, Metallica jumped on a ferry to Sweden to continue their European tour. By this time Hetfield's wrist was almost healed, and he was desperately keen to get back on guitar – which he did, at a gig at Stockholm's Solnhallen. Later that night, the Metallica convoy of two buses left for Copenhagen, which would involve a trip through the Swedish countryside. What happened the following morning was to change Metallica's direction forever.

JAMES HETFIELD

The bus carrying the band swerved off the road between the towns of Ljungby and Varnamo in Sweden. Some parties reported ice on the surface but whatever the cause, the net result was Metallica's tour bus lying on its side by the verge of the E4 road. Obviously a large tour bus full of people and gear is going to fall hard when it lands on its side, but what was not immediately obvious to Hetfield, Ulrich, Hammett and the others who'd crawled out, was that bass player Cliff Burton was still trapped under the bus. It later transpired that Burton's bunk had been adjacent to a window, and the crash had thrown Burton out of that opening.

It seems that the first response from Hetfield was one of anger, as he related in a 1993 interview: "I saw the bus lying right on him. I saw his legs sticking out. I freaked ... Cliff wasn't alive anymore." Shocked and still in his underwear after the crash, Hetfield paced up and down the section road where the bus had skidded, looking for the patch of ice that had seemingly caused the incident. He later stated that he found none. The driver was subsequently determined not at fault for the accident and no charges against him were brought. After all the band members and crew were taken to hospital, the band stayed in a hotel in Llungby where Hetfield immersed his grief in copious alcohol and vented his rage and frustration by smashing hotel room windows while screaming in anger at his friend's death.

The remainder of the European tour was obviously cancelled while the dust settled on the tragically unnecessary loss. Fred Cotton was in touch with Hetfield by post during that European trip. "James wrote me loads of letter from that time on the road, telling me what was happening. I even remember one letter where he actually said he was concerned about the tour bus," as Cotton recalls. "I kept all those letters you know, but when I moved house I lost them all." While Cotton was primarily James's friend, he had also become a good friend of Cliff's, and rated him incredibly highly as a player.

Not only was Burton a supremely gifted musician whose very existence had changed Metallica's direction profoundly, he was also a very likeable and good-hearted twenty-four-year-old man, of whom Hetfield was extremely fond. Burton was not just laid-back in style, but he was also a thinker.

Joel McIver, the British journalist and author of two related books (one of them focusing on Burton), clearly recognises Cliff's significance despite he and James — in theory - having little in common. "Cliff was a punk-loving hippie from a rural SF suburb, while James was a stadium-rock-obsessed boozer from the mean streets of LA. The interesting part of their relationship was that Cliff was older and wiser, and knew more about music theory."

At times, it must have seemed to James Hetfield that all the people close to him were either taken away or left of their own accord. This unavoidable lack of control perhaps added to his desire to control events around him, as we've already acknowledged. In an interview many years later during the band's notorious *Some Kind Of Monster* documentary, Hetfield summed that feeling up rather well: "The way I learned how to love things was just to choke 'em to death. You know, 'Don't go anywhere', 'Don't leave' ... you know, and 'You have to stay here'."

That honest admission of how he dealt with relationships fits in exactly with his behaviour, and while on the surface it may appear controlling — particularly for those on the receiving end perhaps — it's impossible not to feel some sympathy for a guy who at the age of only twenty three knew more than most about loss.

Returning to San Francisco, Metallica were understandably devastated by what had happened in Sweden. They also felt that the best thing to do for the band's future would be to somehow get back out on the road. They were certain that Burton would have actively wanted them to continue, as Hetfield suggested in an MTV interview in 1990: "The last thing Cliff would've wanted us to do was quit. He'd be the first one to kick us in the ass and make us wake up." So wake up they did, and after what they called "a brief yet intense mourning period", the irrepressible Metallica set about sourcing a bass player to replace the somewhat irreplaceable Cliff Burton.

Chapter 8
Jason, Jaymz And Eric

"I really think that Cliff's passing affected James a great deal," Rex Brown reckons. Whoever came in to replace Cliff Burton in Metallica was not going to have an easy time, for two reasons. Firstly, Burton was a complete one-off, and his style and attitude were a crucial feature in the band's music between 1983 and 1986. Secondly, and more importantly, the remaining band members, and particularly James Hetfield, had been hit hard by Cliff's death and had had little real time to grieve his passing. To go out on the road so quickly was brave and there was a hard working logic to it, but there was also a risk they were merely papering over the emotional cracks.

The band used Brian Slagel as a sounding board for hiring a new bass player, and his view was that Joey Vera – from Armored Saint – was the most logical choice. The band already knew him well but at that point in Armored Saint's trajectory, it was a tough decision for Vera, as Slagel explains: "Joey had grown up with all those guys in that band, they were like his brothers." So while Vera was flattered at Metallica's interest, as anyone would be, he wanted to see where Armored Saint would take him, and so politely declined.

Re-enter Eric Braverman. He'd been in and around Tucson, trying to get his metal magazine published when he got a phone call from his friend Joe Lopez telling him to check out a band called Flotsam And Jetsam.

Braverman went to meet this band to do an interview with them for his new magazine: "So I walk in there, and here's this guy called Jason Newsted with glasses on, and [he] has this little note book, trying to be the most professional person he could ever be – because this was his first ever interview." Bear in mind,

Braverman was yet to publish an issue at that point.

After that initial meeting, Braverman and Newsted hit it off pretty good as Eric remembers: "We just started talking a lot and Jason says, 'You're a funny guy, you've got a lot of information. How would you like to help me with my band and write songs with me?'" That's precisely what happened as Eric goes on to say: "I ended up writing songs for him that ended up on *No Place For Disgrace* – Flotsam And Jetsam's first major label album." The friendship continued until September of 1986 when Braverman got a phone call from Newsted saying: "Dude, someone just called me and said Cliff Burton's just died."

Shocked by the tragic news about the guy he'd enjoyed that smoke with back on the *Ride The Lightning* tour, Braverman called Jason back after a couple of days and said: "This is your job." Braverman had also seen Metallica on that summer's tour with Ozzy, and had written down the band's set-list, and put those songs on a tape. "I gave Jason that tape, and told his girlfriend to look after him and make sure he could sit in a room all alone and learn these songs."

Jason listened and learnt the songs as requested. Meanwhile, Braverman had already sown the Newsted seed with label boss Michael Alago, and helped Newsted to fly up to the audition that Alago had set up. "Michael should be given a lot more credit in the Hetfield story," Braverman opines. "He was the first person to say 'James Hetfield is a star', and that was long before he became one."

Not only were the band immediately impressed by Jason's playing – which was already at a very high level – but they also liked his drive and passion, and that was one of the main reasons he fitted in. Jason Newsted was first and foremost a Metallica fan, so he knew how much it meant to be on the brink of joining his favourite band. After a night of drinking at a bar in San Francisco as some kind of initiation, Jason Newsted officially became Metallica's bass player (perhaps understandably the news didn't exactly go down well with his former band-mates in Flotsam and Jetsam, although with hindsight it must have been a decision they could understand. Although their debut album earned the first ever 6K review in *Kerrang!* magazine, they never enjoyed the same commercial success as Metallica).

Newsted wouldn't have a lot of time to dwell on his new position however, because Metallica wanted him to play his first gig for them after he'd rehearsed all the songs to everyone's satisfaction. Eric Braverman got dragged along that night too: "It was an un-announced show at the Country Club in Reseda, supporting Metal Church. Jason wanted me to come and hang out with him and do what I do."

What Braverman 'did' was, as he put it: "Enjoy the whole rock 'n' roll heavy metal genre – that I think should be enjoyed to the fullest, and have boisterous fun which I've been doing ever since." James Hetfield was one guy who certainly didn't initially appreciate Braverman's presence as Eric recalls: "That night at the Country Club, James was saying to Jason, 'Oh, so you're already bringing some Flotsam personnel along with you', and stuff like that, and this is day one. And they were riding him [Jason] about the T-shirt he was wearing. And that kind of thing never stopped."

Braverman remembers Newsted questioning him that night as to why he thought James was treating him like that, and Eric asked Jason to "imagine what it'd be like if you ever disagreed with him. I told him that a hundred times." Sometime down the line, that day would surely come …

Politics aside, Jason performed that night – and at another secret gig the next night in Anaheim – as if his life depended on it. Braverman knows why too. "He performed in the spirit of knowing how lucky he was. He put in twice the energy that they did. It might sound a bit corny, but he wanted to honour Cliff and his fans and family by playing an awesome show every time he went on-stage."

What is worth a little examination however is the early relationship between Eric Braverman and James Hetfield, because it actually reveals quite a lot about Hetfield's personality. Braverman explains: "From the very beginning, I saw a lot of him because I was with Jason. It was always like it was all a bit of a fun challenge. For example, if I was walking down the hall, he'd knock my hat off."

That was the kind of prank Hetfield clearly enjoyed, and given that Braverman wasn't exactly averse to a bout of goofing around himself, it seemed the two had a fair bit in common. "James always liked to challenge me with snide comments and just ridiculous attitude. I actually thought that this guy was becoming a pretty good friend of mine," remembers Eric.

Braverman had made himself something of a fixture at Metallica events, and had also worked his way on to the writing staff of the Metallica fanzine *So What*. "I was given pretty much *carte-blanche* to do whatever the hell I wanted for a few years. Also, in my first *Loud* magazine back in 1985, which had non-heavy bands like Keel and Bon Jovi in it, I put James Hetfield – who looks like he's fifteen – on the cover."

Braverman was always very keen to put forward fun ideas for the band in the fanzine and that inevitably brought him closer to James. "I always just saw him as this guy who'd got put in this situation, we had a good rapport and when we were interfacing we'd challenge each other because we were enjoying each other's sense of humour."

The relationship was a strange one, and one that Hetfield always kept at arm's length, as Braverman confirms: "I'd always hang out with him because I was with Jason, but it never got to the stage where I could call him or something."

With little chance to get to know his band-mates and settle-in, Newsted and Metallica headed for a brief tour of Japan. The tour was a success in that it introduced Jason to the band's audience, but in an understated way. His obvious talent saw him fit in seamlessly with the live show. But it was also a trying time for Newsted given that Ulrich and particularly Hetfield used it for a series of grim initiation ceremonies, all designed to test their new guy's stick-ability. Hetfield and Ulrich didn't bargain on Newsted's durability however, nor did they figure that their target even understood the psychology behind his plight.

What Newsted understood perfectly – which consequently made Hetfield and Ulrich's actions less hurtful – was the simple fact that it wasn't in any way personal. Perhaps all Newsted represented was a 'somebody' in a place that was formerly occupied by Cliff, therefore he merely became the most accessible object for their grief and frustration.

Hetfield, Ulrich and Hammett buried their grief and emotion

under a fire-blanket called Metallica, and periodically over time, flames would lick out from underneath, only to be quickly stamped out again. In reality Jason was an excellent musician, and an extremely intelligent, thoughtful man, but most of all he was a fighter, and it would be that quality that he'd need to call on most frequently during the first five years of his tenure in the band.

After that quick stint in Japan, Metallica returned to the US for tour dates on the East coast and Canada, before finishing up in San Francisco on January 2,1987. The band then had to go back to Europe to honour new dates that were created to compensate for the shows they'd had to cancel after the bus crash. Again, they'd go back to Zwolle to play at the Aardshok festival, alongside aforementioned Swiss thrashers Celtic Frost. The band did have further live commitments but they wouldn't be until the summer and in the meantime they were working on putting out their first video.

For a band who at that time was the very antithesis of your average MTV act, it would have been surprising if what they'd come up with had been a polished, heavily edited feature. *Cliff 'Em All,* as it was called, was anything but polished or heavily edited. In fact it was positively grimy and un-edited, and featured hand-held camera filmed moments from Cliff Burton's era in the band.

Most of the footage was fan's material, and the rest was personal to the band or crew. Hetfield had written some notes of his own on the cover and the whole thing had the feel of a bootleg, which was completely intentional. Hetfield's notes were amusing to say the least, summed up by the words, "The quality in some places ain't that happening, but the feeling is there and that's what matters!!!" He then signed off as 'Jaymz', a pseudonym he'd use for many years in fanzines and other written messages to the fans.

Initially it looked like this was Hetfield's disclaimer for the band releasing a video at all. But on closer inspection, his words were close to a touching public tribute to Cliff. It did however give clues that there was a sensitive side in there, and that in the right – or maybe the wrong circumstances – that would come to the surface. The fact that the video sold so heavily confirmed that Hetfield's sentiments had resonated with the fans. The short answer was that they 'got' it, and *Cliff 'Em All* is an extremely worthy addition to any fan's collection.

That spring, the band was in San Francisco, and predictably James was back with his buddy Fred Cotton – taking it easy before the summer festival appearances. Meanwhile Lars and Jason were fixing up a garage in a house Ulrich had just bought, with a view to making it into a private rehearsal space.

John Kornarens, who was still a good friend, came up and helped with the DIY work that was needed to make the place useable. "Jason was pretty good at that stuff, and when James was around he was okay too," Kornarens recalls. You would have thought that moving stuff around in a garage and the use of power tools might have proved more dangerous than hanging out having fun, but it was Hetfield who presented the band with their next issue, and it was a problem that was becoming rather familiar. As the story goes, Hetfield, Cotton, Hammett and a couple of others had gone up to Oakland hills to hang around playing with skateboards. Cotton remembers the details: "We were at this empty swimming pool at this old abandoned hotel and we were skating again. James got up a little too high as usual!"

When Hetfield came down, things weren't good. "I heard his arm snap and James shouted, 'Oh fuck! It's broke!' I had to take him to Highland Hospital in Oakland which is just a county hospital and is in a [tough neighbourhood], but it was the closest one," recalls Cotton.

Imagine the scene: Fred Cotton and James Hetfield in Oakland's County hospital with James's arm at strange angles. "We went in and he was alright, but he had a compound fracture and his bone had popped out of his arm. The nurse came out and said, 'He wants you in here with him,' and I was teasing him because they had him hooked up to IVs and shit."

Apparently James appeared to have another elbow in his wrist area where there shouldn't be one – never a good state of affairs. "He screamed out in pain and the nurse had to take this long cue-tip to make sure that it was the bone that had made the cut, so she stuck it all the way in his arm," Cotton remembers. After that they gave him some drugs and did the surgery to fix the break and very soon James was fooling around, as Cotton recalls: "He was fine and recovering, flicking boogers at the wall and shit."

Obviously the several weeks it would take for Hetfield's arm to heal meant that the band couldn't really do any serious rehearsal for new material as planned. So instead, they opted for a stop-gap project, which would appear as an EP of cover versions (called *The $5.98 EP*). Most of the tracks chosen were by bands that had influenced or inspired Metallica at some point, and the production sounded like they were playing in *your* front room, far less theirs – which was the desired effect. It really is that live and energetic, and you can actually here Hetfield's fingers grating on the strings while he chisels out some truly awesome riffs.

The first selection would be a track called 'Helpless' by NWOBHM pioneers (and Lars's friends) Diamond Head. To say it's stunning would be an understatement. The original version was a decent song – albeit that it was performed at roughly half this velocity – but Hetfield's precision riffing is as astounding as it's ever been, and the monstrous rhythm section of Ulrich and Jason 'Newkid' Newsted as he'd been dubbed, is equally compelling.

Next is 'The Small Hours' by British band Holocaust (remember John Kornaren's warped copy?) and on this track, outright velocity is replaced by sheer heaviness. It really works a treat though. Killing Joke's 'The Wait' follows, and it was surprising that it was left off UK versions of the EP, particularly as Killing Joke are a distinctly British band, both in sound and ideology. It's a good interpretation though – featuring a muddy sounding central riff and Hetfield's sinister vocal delivery. Newsted's rumbling bass introduces the solid crunch of 'Crash Course In Brain Surgery', originally performed by Budgie. Again, listen out for Hetfield's complex picking, there's much more going on there than you on first listen.

The final offering is really two tracks, composed of a medley of two tunes by punk band The Misfits called 'Last Caress' and 'Green Hell'. Apparently it had been the late Cliff Burton who'd alerted Hetfield to The Misfits aggressive style and horror movie imagery. The manner in which these two punk tracks are dispatched with such consummate ease – particularly by Hetfield – was indicative of the band's overall versatility of course, but also of the thin line that existed between thrash metal and punk as a genre.

The EP carried the subtitle *Garage Days Revisited*, and was recorded in no time at all – at least by Metallica's standards – at A&M and Conway studios in LA (after Ted Nugent was persuaded to vacate the place for the six days that Metallica needed). It hit the shops on August 21, 1987 to rave reviews. The sleeve, like the *Cliff 'Em All* video, featured a scrawled note to the fans, explaining the rather laid-back ideology behind this excellent EP.

The band were due to return to Donington that month for the Monsters Of Rock festival they'd played at two years previously, and to warm-up they played a secret gig at London's 100 Club, under the distinctly un-secret sobriquet 'Damage, Inc'.

Suffice to say, there were sufficiently more Metallica fans in London who saw through the secret name than there was space for in this rather intimate venue. Less intimate was the vast throng that turned up at Donington to see Metallica appear on the bill alongside Bon Jovi, who themselves were flying unfeasibly high on the gazillion-selling *Slippery When Wet* – an overtly commercial slew of pomp-rock anthems which was mixed by a Canadian sound engineer and producer called Bob Rock.

Despite the obvious stylistic difference between the two main bands, the festival was a success, if for no other reason than that it promoted Metallica's recent EP rather effectively. One more festival appearance at a show in Nuremberg supporting classic rock gods Deep Purple ended Metallica's commitments for the year, and at that point the four members dispersed to start giving thought to material for their fourth album.

Chapter 9

Doris

James Hetfield and Metallica had a considerable chunk of time off in the latter part of 1987, so the band went their separate ways to relax and live life, prior to re-grouping to take stock of their next move. "This was the only time we'd really get to see James and the guys. They had become such road dogs; they were hardly ever in town," Ron Quintana remembers.

During this somewhat extended hiatus, each member would work on their own ideas from riff tapes that would later represent their contribution towards their next album. Riff tapes were how Hetfield, Ulrich, Hammett and now Newsted did things. What this meant was that each player – who probably had some kind of home recording space – would commit any ideas, riffs or fully formed songs onto tape, in order that they could listen to them all later and keep the good stuff for the record, while the remainder would be stored away for future use or perhaps discarded. Historically, mainly Hetfield and Ulrich's material made the cut, but on occasion several contributions from others would sneak under the radar. Jason Newsted was a keen composer of new material however, and he made himself busy doing that – while occasionally hanging out with his buddy Eric Braverman.

James was living with his girlfriend during these autumn months in an apartment in Talbot Street, El Cerrito. In his free time he was hanging out with pals like Fred Cotton, as well as other friends like Jim and Lou Martin.

Jim was a friend of the late Cliff Burton's, and also a member of the Spastik Children project that both James and Cliff had endorsed in recent years. He would also play bass in the alternative metal giants Faith No More before leaving in 1993. James liked to hang out with the Martins, drink beer and mess around.

As 1987 dragged on, the specifics of Metallica's fourth studio album were increasingly fresh on the agenda, and one of those specifics up for discussion was who should produce it. Again, there was no problem whatsoever with the job Flemming Rasmussen had done on *Master Of Puppets*, and its huge success and timeless longevity are ample testimony to that fact.

Unfortunately – as can often happen in the record industry – Rasmussen was already committed to another project at the time (a band bizarrely called Danish Pregnant Woman in fact) so Metallica reluctantly had to look for someone new, and had a good idea who that might be.

Earlier that year, a producer called Mike Clink had been involved with a monstrously successful, and now legendary album by LA sleaze-rockers Guns N' Roses. That album, entitled *Appetite For Destruction*, had crushed all in its path while also throwing up several singles, of which 'Sweet Child O' Mine' was the commercial zenith. Not only was *Appetite* a great mixture of raw, sleazy tunes, it also sounded fantastic – with a bass-led rumble which really gave the songs some added power.

None of this was lost on Hetfield and Ulrich either, and they really liked the way the album sounded, not to mention the frightening sales figures it hastily accrued. With that in mind, they made a decision to hire Clink to produce their fourth record that would be called ... *And Justice For All*. Apparently, most of the songs were pretty well written before the assigned date to enter the studio on January 19,1988, and it promised to be another major leap forward.

In an interview with *Music And Sound Output* in 1988, Hetfield and Ulrich explained their processes: "We've got riffs from years and years," explained Hetfield. "On the road we constantly riff and write it down." That material is then sifted and divided into individual categories as Hetfield continues: "Like, some shit is strong enough to be the main idea of a tune. Then we go through the tapes and try to find possible bridges, choruses, middle bits or whatever. After we have a skeleton of a song, we start getting a feel for what the song is really like. Then we search for a title from a list of titles that fits with the riffing's mood." Pretty disciplined stuff actually, and thereafter, Hetfield's 'songs' are almost at the demo stage and ready to record; sessions were booked for One On One Studios in LA.

Right from the beginning there was a complication and according to Lars that seemed to be all the ancillary distractions that go with being in an LA studio as opposed to one in Copenhagen. "You walk in there and there's eight secretaries, computers and fuckin' fax machines. I know the stuff is necessary but there comes a point where it's too much," he told *Music And Sound Output.*

The studio surroundings weren't the only issue however, because these Clink sessions never really got off the ground, to the point where Ulrich put in a call to Rasmussen asking him to reconsider – he flew to LA a fortnight later.

"The major change as far as I knew was that they'd got these all new *Mesa Boogie* amps for the guitars, and I know that there were a lot of difficulties getting the right guitar sound. And [the band] didn't really resolve that until I got there," Flemming Rasmussen remembers.

Seemingly, when Rasmussen arrived at One On One, he stripped down the equipment that Clink had been using and started all over again, using some old gear that was lying around the studio. "I also had an equalizer inserted on the actual amp so that I could change the guitar sound from the control room," Flemming adds.

Further details as to why Metallica and Mike Clink didn't hit off are not available. But there is an irony here. Metallica back off working with a commercially-orientated producer, only to end up later with Bob Rock, one of the most commercially successful producers in the world.

To Hetfield at least, recent events illustrated to him that the band just couldn't at that point work with anyone apart from Rasmussen. "Well we can, but it's a slow process," Hetfield told *Music And Sound Output.* So, Rasmussen and Metallica recorded the new album at One On One and surfaced sometime in May with a record that just needed mixing. Shortly afterwards, James flew up to San Francisco to visit Fred Cotton in Pinole for a while – before they went out on the Van Halen-headlined

Monsters Of Rock tour.

"James came up to visit and my sister had to book him a hotel room because he didn't have any ID," Cotton vividly recalls. Hetfield also had a cassette tape with him, of the recorded but as yet un-mixed ... *And Justice For All.* "The one he brought me had no vocal tracks on it, and I said 'This is done?', it was as heavy as hell." As Fred remembers. "I was fucking blown away at how it sounded."

One on-going source of speculation about the new record was the levels – namely very low – of the bass. This issue of how ... *And Justice For All* sounded would re-surface intermittently over the years, without any clear indication of why the bass guitar ended up so low in the mix. It would be foolish to ignore that suggestions were made alleging it was an intentional move to downplay Newsted's role, but that would seem unlikely given how prominent his parts had been on the EP which represented his recording debut. Newsted *was* one who did feel that it was intentional, and went as far as to say so in that notorious *Playboy* interview in 2001. In defence of both Hetfield and Ulrich, however, much of the *AJFA* process took place while the band were on the road – a fact which both Hetfield and Ulrich have suggested might have dulled their senses a little when it came to the sound they ultimately wanted. Secondly, and this is key: Newsted's bass parts at that early time were comparatively simple, and in many cases involved mirroring the rhythm guitar track; hence the rather indistinct sound. Whatever happened, and whatever the reasons were, *...And Justice For All* does sound unusual.

Lonn Friend, at that time the executive editor of *RIP* magazine – the first non-porn title published by the iconic pornographer Larry Flynt – was at the box office of The Roxy on Sunset Boulevard one night in late 1987, waiting to see 'some obscure band'. Across the lobby he spotted two long-haired guys standing and talking.

"Hey, you're James and Lars from Metallica," Friend remembers announcing. "I introduced myself and Lars recognised my name from an article I'd written for a men's magazine about porn films in Paris. James laughed and suggested that we blow the band off and head next door to the Rainbow for a beer, which we did, and we spent the next couple of hours talking, connecting. They told me they were in Hollywood recording their album ... *And Justice For All*."

Friend was completely stunned by Hetfield's modest persona at the time. "My first impression of James was *Here's a musician who keeps himself to himself and lets his music do his talking.*"While Ulrich apparently did a lot of the talking that night, James also played his part too: "James would toss in a quick-witted one liner here and there. He was authentic, didn't give any signals he was in a rock band, far less a very successful one," Friend recalls, clearly impressed – and more than a little surprised.

Whatever the exact circumstances surrounding the mixed levels of Newsted's bass parts, the finished product's legacy would be the songs, and fortunately, ... *And Justice For All* is for many listeners (the author included) the band's most compelling listen, even allowing for the rather bizarre sonic experience it serves up.

Any initial misgivings about the bone-dry mix are quickly dispelled by opening track 'Blackened', whose menacing intro oozes from the speakers – fading-in amid a dual guitar wail that suggests nothing but impending, cataclysmic doom.

As it happens, that's what the song is about too – the ruin and ultimate decay of planet Earth. As that intro ends, Ulrich's drums engage – ahead of a clinically potent Hetfield riff which slows to a mid-tempo pace for the verse. It's far more technical than any previous material and Hetfield's vocals are a further notch up the 'angry scale' than even *Master Of Puppets*. As an opener it's as good as anything they've attempted as well as an intelligent commentary from Hetfield about the long-term viability of the planet.

This intelligent lyrical commentary was not lost on peers like Kreator's Mille Petrozza: "I love some of his lyrics on ... *And Justice For All*. It's my favourite album of theirs, and James stuff has a very smart and critical undertone."

Petrozza is correct of course, as thematically the entire album questions the true value, and indeed existence of the concept of justice, and the title track that comes next encapsulates it all with a running time of almost ten minutes. During that period it twists and turns like an angry serpent, but always adheres to generally the same feel and theme. While sometimes criticised for being too clever for its own good, it remains a monument to the development of the band at that time and would become their progressive masterpiece, as well as being the last time they'd deliver a track of such an overtly complex nature.

Anyone that thought James Hetfield had reached his lyrical high point on the band's previous album obviously hadn't bargained for the depth and just sheer clever use of words he manages on this entire piece of work. "He is a masterful, underrated wordsmith. It's crazy! It's like 'How did you do that?!'" Eric Braverman says while assessing Hetfield's lyrics.

'Eye Of The Beholder' is next, and is without doubt the album's black sheep. Again, it has a fade-in intro, but the weird riff that surfaces initially is much more akin to a mainstream metal band like Dokken than that of the progressive thrash lords Metallica. It's a strange beast really, with a pounding, almost tribal Ulrich drum pattern, but Hetfield's acerbic lyrical assault makes it utterly essential listening.

The track that comes next, simply entitled 'One', is the token 'quiet' (initially at least) track, and its significance will always be that it hastened the band's first bigger budget video to accompany it. Sonically, it's a close relative of both 'Fade To Black' and 'Welcome Home (Sanitarium)' from the previous two albums, the tortured tale of a war survivor left only with his torso and head – a state of questionable authenticity when you think about it. Ushered in by the horrific sounds of war, it builds on a gorgeous, cleanly picked guitar intro punctuated by Ulrich's snare cracks. The tempo ups towards the end – clearly mirroring the increasing angst of the unfortunate limbless subject – before 'One' climaxes with a blast of guitars, drums. Bass ... not so much.

'Shortest Straw' is next, and on first listen it is actually quite forgettable, but over time it's probably one of the tracks that endures best on the whole album – an opinion that Ulrich himself has been heard to share. It's another progressively complex affair, but one that really would have benefitted from a more sympathetic mix – it's just too dry and claustrophobic.

Similarly oppressive is the lead single from the album entitled

'Harvester of Sorrow' – the harrowing tale of a father who reputedly slaughters his family for no obvious reason other than his own dwindling sanity. It's certainly a strange choice for a single, and possesses a similarly lumbering tempo as a track like 'The Thing That Should Not Be' from two years earlier. Fans of the band got the opportunity to hear it well in advance of the actual album's release – given it was aired at many of the Monsters Of Rock shows – and as such it has always been something of a live favourite.

The complex 'Frayed Ends Of Sanity' follows and is a track that receives little or no comment, either negative or positive. Nevertheless it's a fine addition, with an extremely unusual intro section with weird Oompa-Loompa-type vocal harmonies. As has been the pattern, there is an instrumental track (if you discount the few lines of Hetfield speaking) and it's a remnant of Cliff Burton's riff writing entitled rather prophetically 'To Live Is To Die'. Its lilting, cleanly picked intro builds through a jagged, stop–start riff until the first solo by Hammett leads into a triumphant dual guitar section. This then suddenly cuts to an achingly touching clean passage that is soon decorated by what is probably one of James Hetfield's all-time best lead guitar solos. On a purely technical level it's relatively modest. In terms of raw emotion and just sheer propriety it's everything however, and you can almost hear Hetfield thinking about what note should come next. Suffice to say he chooses the right one – as he always seems to. It's sublime, and almost miss-able if you're not listening closely enough.

The final track on ... *And Justice For All* is an utter gem, punctuated by the torrent of pure bile and frustration which exits James Hetfield's mouth. Called simply 'Dyer's Eve', it's one of the more obvious lyrical rants about his upbringing that Hetfield has ever committed to record, all carried along by a riff that's just insanely fast and precision-picked by the perpetrator himself. This track, more than probably any other in the Metallica canon, perhaps illustrates Hetfield's level of emotion, and in many ways it seems to be a rather cathartic exercise, as he never really goes quite this far again. Many of the words that he says can be theoretically linked to his own experiences, and the fact that it's accompanied by one of his most brutally exhilarating riffs only makes it more telling and plausible.

As a package ... *And Justice For All* was a very well-rounded progressive metal record, with a staggering attention to detail that more than made up for its unfortunate sonic failings. To the general public it would still be tarred with a broad thrash metal brush, but for devoted fans of both the band and real thrash, ... *And Justice For All* was definitely a subtle move towards the mainstream.

The sleeve featured cover art by Brian 'Pushead' Schroeder, and depicted Lady Justice bound in chains and blindfolded. In the tour that would follow, 'Doris', as she would be nicknamed, would be an integral part of the stage set, and her crumbling form a symbol of failed justice.

As was mentioned previously, Metallica had already been touring the US since May as part of the huge Monsters Of Rock extravaganza, which featured bands like Van Halen, Led Zeppelin-influenced Kingdom Come and middle-of-the-road rockers Dokken.

Hetfield confirmed the party atmosphere in an interview with *Metal Hammer* magazine: "That was the Jagermeister days. I am still hearing stories about it, like that I slugged Lars but I don't remember any of it ... we were very much into drinking and having a good fucking time."

While the band were out of control on tour, their previous album *Master Of Puppets* was being confirmed Platinum, an achievement which must have surely augured well for sales of a new record that was going to be pushed significantly harder as a result of an increasingly wide-reaching touring regime. Throughout their career, Metallica have always been one of metal's most relentless and hard-working live acts.

When ... *And Justice For All* was eventually released on September 5, 1988, the band were already in a serious touring groove which was great preparation for their own trek called simply 'Damaged Justice', which began in Europe six days later. Meanwhile, the critics' response to the album was almost entirely positive too: "Thrash is too demeaning a term for this metametal, a marvel of precision channelled aggression," *Rolling Stone* reckoned.

Dates in mainland Europe followed by a further fourteen in the UK and Ireland – with support provided by ex-Misfits member Glen Danzig's namesake band – gave European audiences ample opportunity to absorb live versions of the new material that was received extremely well (a fact the author can confirm, having attended two of the shows). Further gigs in Europe, with support now provided by intelligent metallers Queensryche, finished the band's European tour on November 5, and led into a week-long break prior to the demanding US leg of the tour. During that break, Hetfield was back in San Francisco briefly, and even managed to call in at one of his old haunts the Stone to see Mille Petrozza's Kreator play a gig there. "Someone told me James was there, and before we went on-stage the band were all excited!" Petrozza laughs. "But we never got the chance to meet."

It wasn't all free time however, as the band used the opportunity to record the aforementioned video for second single 'One', having edited its eight-minute-plus bulk to suit. It wasn't to be a standard 'live' performance-type video featuring the band on-stage however, nor was it to be a 'Hollywood' piece with scantily clad models pawing at the band's pelvic areas.

What it turned out to be was a rather depressing clip featuring footage of the hapless, and for that matter limb-less war veteran writhing on a hospital bed, while the band themselves grimly thrashed away in what looked like a dimly lit warehouse. Hardly your standard MTV fare, and far from a commercial sell-out either.

1988 became 1989 and the 'Damaged Justice' tour continued through the Mid-West at a glacial crawl, while the album sold by the cartload on the back of it. A little surprisingly perhaps, Metallica were nominated for a Grammy in February of 1989, in the category of 'Best Heavy Metal Performance'. However, the band were bizarrely edged out by prehistoric folk-rock act Jethro Tull who, apart from not being a true heavy metal act, didn't even have an album out at the time.

Completely unfazed, Metallica's US tour ground on and on in March and April until Queensryche left the bill, but not before James had organised Chippendale-type dancers to invade the stage

Performing with Obsession, his first proper band, formed in 1978.
Photo: Ron McGovney

James and Ron McGovney become faux *Hit Parader*
cover stars inside a fairground photobooth, 1981.
Photo: From the archive of Ron McGovney

With pictures of The Scorpions and Michael Schenker on the wall,
James strikes a rebellious pose, 1981.
Photo: Ron McGovney

Cliff and James onstage in 1981.
Photo: Larry Hulst/Michael Ochs Archives/Getty Images

Aardschok Festival February 11, 1984: Lars, Cliff and Hetfield.
Photo: Pete Cronin/Redferns/Getty Images

Hanging out with friends – in the picture are
Jason Newsted, Lou Martin, James Hetfield and Fred Cotton.
Photo: Eric Braverman

James at Jason Newsted's house after a Flotsam And Jetsam show in
San Francisco, with Mike Gilbert, Lou Martin and Brad Halverson.
Photo: Eric Braverman

Hetfield hams it up to the camera at Jason Newsted's house,
shortly after Jason joined the band in 1987.
Photo: Eric Braverman

Kirk Hammet's bachelor party in 1987 (l-r): Journalist and Metallica
fanzine editor Steffan Chirazi, Hetfield, Hammett and Eric Braverman.
Photo: Eric Braverman

Songwriting mid-air, circa 1992.
Photo: Bernhard Kuhmstedt/Retna

Backstage at the LA Forum in 1992: James with friend
and former Norwalk housemate Ron McGovney
during the seemingly endless 'Black' album tour.
Photo: Ron McGovney

Backstage at the Oakland Coliseum, September 24, 1992.
Photo: John Storey / Time Life Pictures / Getty Images

The difference two decades make: (top) Hetfield at Castle Donington for
Monsters of Rock, 1987 and (bottom) returning for the *Download Festival* 2006.
Photos: George Chin/Iconicpix

Friends Reunited: Michael Alago, who signed the band to the
Elektra label in 1984, hangs out with his old friend backstage
at Madison Square Garden on November 14, 2009.
Photo: Michael Alago

during Queensryche's set on the last night (Queensryche singer Geoff Tate reportedly didn't see the funny side of the joke). Metallica then headed to New Zealand to be supported on the Australasian leg by rock band The Cult. Shows in Hawaii, Japan and Alaska brought the tour back to Canada before swinging through the Mid-West like a whirlwind of metal unstoppability.

Somebody significant who caught up with the 'Damaged Justice' tour when they rolled into Vancouver was producer Bob Rock, who at that time was about to help resurrect Mötley Crüe's wobbling career by producing their career best offering entitled *Dr Feelgood*. In the same way that Mike Clink had given *Appetite For Destruction* a beefy bass-led sound, Rock would do exactly the same kind of job with *Dr Feelgood*, and that was a fact that wouldn't be lost on Hetfield and Ulrich when they heard that record.

Rock actually introduced himself to the band that night in Vancouver, and was seemingly blown away by Metallica's live sound. He told them that in his opinion they had not come even vaguely close to capturing that energy on record. That information – as you could probably imagine – didn't initially go down very well with Hetfield and Ulrich, but at the same time a seed of doubt was sown as to the band's next direction – albeit that ... *And Justice For All* had been a resounding commercial and creative success, peaking at Number 6 on the *Billboard* Chart.

Also on the Canadian leg of proceedings, Dan Beehler of Exciter got the chance to hook up with James again. "They came to my home town of Ottawa and it was great. He's got that big smile, and they treated me awesome that night." While Metallica were without doubt a different band from those basement days in Baker Street, Beehler was pleasantly surprised by how little James had changed personally. "He hadn't changed at all. As soon as he saw me it was like the old days. I guess he has a soft spot for people from his past."

When the 'Damaged Justice' tour eventually came to an exhausted end, after a draining period of time on the road, Hetfield and Ulrich completely dropped off most people's radars until early in 1990, when it was announced they'd contribute a cover version of Motörhead's 'Stone Cold Crazy' to an Elektra label compilation. Apart from a February appearance at the

JAMES HETFIELD

Grammy's where the band picked up an award for the 'One' video, very little was heard from the band for the next three months, and given the exhaustive nature of recording and touring ... *And Justice For All*, that was no particular surprise.

Chapter 10

Liberty Or Death

To suggest that the early 1990s were a pivotal point for rock music would be a huge understatement. It was a fulcrum, a watershed, whatever you want to call it, and it was also a period that would see some relatively well-known bands simply not survive, or be forced to operate from a position deep underground.

The early 1990s would also be a critical era for Hetfield and Metallica too, despite the fact that they'd reached a much larger demographic of the music public with ... *And Justice For All* (which was a miracle when taking into account that it was still a relatively extreme bunch of songs for many people's tastes). However, suddenly there was a new 'scene' on the horizon; to continue down the line of the previous record's overtly complex and progressive path could well have resulted in Metallica being isolated along with other similar bands, by the movement that was sweeping American music – grunge.

Originating in Seattle, grunge was an amalgam of rock's attitude and punk's rebellion, melded into a depressingly weary mixture, performed in a fairly humourless manner. Nonetheless, it spread like a stubborn rash through Seattle with early exponents like Soundgarden, Alice In Chains and of course Nirvana initially leading the way.

Jerry Cantrell was one of the founding members of Alice In Chains, and to him grunge was a tag that was retrospective: "We were there before that word was even invented. I don't know if any of the bands were particularly comfortable with that title, but that became the catchphrase that encompassed us all. As far as I saw it, we were all just rock 'n' roll bands to some degree."

A twist of fate that definitely did not harm this new genre's expansion was the eleventh-hour inclusion of Alice In Chains on the thrash metal arena super-tour called 'Clash Of The Titans'. Kicking off the US leg in May 1991, the bill included Slayer, Megadeth and Anthrax, with support from Alice In Chains as a late replacement for Bay Area thrash act Death Angel (who had suffered an horrific bus crash).

Although Alice In Chains stuck out like a sore thumb on such an overtly thrash line-up – and received all manner of abuse from certain sections of the fans – their presence did serve to promote grunge's credentials to arena-sized audiences. Gradually, as the monster tour ground on, Alice In Chains began to win some fans over, and by the time 'Clash Of The Titans' rumbled to a grinding halt in mid-July, grunge was a concept that was definitely on many people's radars.

Whether the style of grunge was actually anything strictly ground-breaking is irrelevant to this book; it was a movement that gathered commercial pace at an alarming rate with the net result that metal – and certainly thrash metal – would soon be completely marginalised by this new fad. Worrying too was the fact that while metal acts unwittingly helped their grunge sidekicks by occasionally taking them out on tour, this was a favour which would not always be returned, as Anthrax's Scott Ian told audiences on the popular documentary entitled *Get Thrashed*: "These grunge types were so narrow minded, you'd never get them taking a metal band out on tour."

While the full extent of the grunge revolution would not become fully apparent until late 1991, the signs were definitely there the preceding year, and Hetfield and Ulrich were very aware of them while taking a break prior to renewed recording activity for album number five.

No previous Metallica album had been commenced without a long and protracted debate about who would produce it, but this time things were a little more clear-cut, and also a bit more controversial. It was no secret that the band collectively recognised the work Bob Rock had done with a whole raft of commercially-minded bands, and it would not be stretching things to suggest that Rock had something akin to a Midas touch, except that he traded a touch of gold for one of pure Platinum – in a sales sense at least.

Even James Hetfield had to grudgingly admit his liking for

Rock's sound: "If you go back and look at the stuff he's produced, it sounds great, even though the songs were crap ..." Hetfield was quoted as saying in Chris Ingham's *Metallica: The Stories Behind The Biggest Songs*. Hammett, who was a life-long fan of The Cult, loved what Rock had done with their successful album *Sonic Temple*, which had made its way into the living rooms and car stereo's of the world on the back of Rock's monster production. In addition, Ulrich just loved Rock's work, period.

All of that combined meant that Metallica had collectively decided Bob Rock would at the very least mix their new album when that time came. The problem was that Rock wanted more. "I didn't really want to mix it", Rock told the *Classic Album* series, and "I actually wanted to produce it." The problem was, Richie Sambora – guitarist with Bon Jovi with whom Rock already had strong connections – wanted him to oversee his debut solo album *Stranger In This Town*.

This gave Rock something of an awkward dilemma. According to music legend, Rock and his family were driving through the Nevada desert on vacation and saw a guy sitting by the side of the road, in the middle of nowhere, wearing a Metallica t-shirt, and that bizarre sign convinced him that Metallica was a project he simply could not turn down. Consequently, Sambora was told the unfortunate news that someone else would have to produce his record.

After a quiet 1990 for Hetfield and the rest of Metallica, recording began at One On One studios sometime in early October with Bob Rock overseeing proceedings. In the *Classic Albums* DVD even Bob Rock acknowledges the band's hesitancy to move away from the security and familiarity of working in the decidedly regimented way they had previously. To say that this would be a new working dynamic would be a huge understatement for Hetfield in particular, given his former dominant role in a studio environment – this new set-up was going to test both his patience and that constant perfectionist's desire to be in control.

Predictably perhaps, things did not initially go well, and for the first three months of recording, Hetfield put Rock – with assistance from his band-mates – through a series of tests. In the same way that they had sounded-out Newsted back in 1987, they were now doing the same thing. Gradually though – and because Rock chose to roll with Hetfield's frequent psychological punches – the band started to enjoy the processes which they were being made to adhere to.

Where on previous albums each band member had recorded their parts alone, on this record Rock was keen that they all played together at times in the studio – thus giving the songs much more of a live feel. In the past the mechanism of recording had by their own admission become very stiff, but now with almost a 'fifth band member' in Rock, there was a much more relaxed feel about the songs, if not the personal relationships.

What Rock did do was to let each facet of the band express itself fully (including Newsted's bass presence as it happened) and the resulting freedom encouraged all the very best abilities of the members, particularly perhaps Hetfield, to flow in a way that they never had before.

Lonn Friend, who was still working with *RIP* magazine, was lucky enough to be invited into the secret environment of One On One studios to report on the band's progress for the magazine's readers. "I got to examine the recording process from a very intimate point of view during the winter of 1990 and spring of 1991," Lonn explains. "I brought our audience the inside story. One night James took me into what he called his 'Tent of Doom' which was his tongue-in-cheek name of the area which housed the mics responsible for picking up that classic Hetfield guitar sound," Friend remembers with more than a touch of awe.

Be in no doubt, this album would have the Hetfield stamp all over it, perhaps more than any record previously. "He showed me the lyrics that night, scrawlings of what would become the theme, heart and soul of that Earth-shaking record," the effusive Friend remembers. "There was a process to the making of that record, Lars and Bob Rock were key players, architects, holders of the script ... but it was James and his musical genius that fed the monster as it grew." Despite all the pressure of delivering this monster, Lonn remembers how approachable James was throughout: "His personality was always humorous, rarely aloof. You could see there was a method to his madness/genius."

While Bob Rock produced with the band, Randy Staub was involved in much of the recording process. Their assistant Mike Tacci – who spent the same nine months with the band too – kindly spoke to the author for this book. Tacci's a very intelligent and talented engineer who would go on to work on records by Megadeth and Lynch Mob among others, and he recognised the genius of Hetfield immediately. "I was working with him for nine months and although I'd worked with other rock and metal bands, I was very, very impressed. James was very confident, and his musical timing was impeccable. Not just that, his lyrics were on a higher and deeper level than I'd come across, and to me he was the core of the band." Like Lonn Friend, Tacci could not help separating the 'business' Hetfield from James the person, and his findings were almost identical. "James was just so down-to-earth and real. He was witty too, and a pleasure and inspiration to be around."

After such glowing testimony from individuals who were physically present at these album sessions, there is little point in further analysis of the actual making of the monster album, which would simply be called *Metallica*. People seem to struggle with eponymous records however, and *Metallica* quickly became referred to as the 'Black' album, simply on account of its plain black cover with a barely discernable band logo, and an image of a coiled rattlesnake.

According to Hetfield, the title – and in fact the plain cover – were a deliberate attempt to channel the listener's attention to the music and not towards any fancy, distracting cover art; an approach that would only succeed if the songs were very good. Fortunately, they were not just good, they were absolutely astounding, and from the moment *Metallica* landed on August 12, 1991, rock music would literally never be the same again. Amazingly, people queued at record stores all over the US on the night before release day, and that frenzied buying behaviour translated to an unprecedented 600,000 unit sales in the first week in the US alone.

What was so amazing about the record was not necessarily that it was so different from anything the band had done before, but much more that it somehow succeeded in fusing the best aspects of the past with something fresh and somehow futuristic. Gone were the complex and progressive sections and the ten-minute running times. These were now replaced with shorter, more overtly traditional verse/chorus arrangements, which crucially incorporated some big, juicy hooks – the kind that regular people could sing in the car or the shower at that.

While die-hard fans would inevitably bitch about the band 'going soft' or 'selling out', anyone with an iota of sense would recognise that *Metallica* was the record the band simply *had* to make; not just that, for a music industry that was approaching a crossroads, it was definitely the right record at the right time. "It took me a while to really get it," Pantera's Rex Brown admits. "Maybe even two years. After that I realised it was a fuckin' great record. I do think that a few kids felt short-changed by that record at first."

It did no harm that the album kicked off with what would be voted by *Kerrang!* magazine's readers in later years as 'The Best Metal Song Of All-Time' – 'Enter Sandman'. Whether that is strictly accurate is open to endless debate, but what is certain is that it had all the attributes of a massive rock song with a hard edge. Beginning with that familiar haunting intro, the classic song soon launches into that memorable three-part circular riff that, as *Rolling Stone*'s David Fricke suggested, "Blew out the speakers on the radio." Hetfield's vocal parts are instantly more harmonious than we've ever heard, while his guitar input is ultra-powerful. Lyrically, it's a little more light-hearted if anything, focusing on the stuff of kid's nightmares – monsters under the bed etc.

The mighty stomp of 'Sad But True' is next and is, as the band's manager Cliff Burnstein once described it, "Music to pull teeth to." Interestingly, its lazy, laid-low riff was a subject of continual discussion in the studio, and it was Rock's suggestion to slow it down that really worked perfectly. Track three, the thrusting 'Holier Than Thou' was originally going to be the lead single, until Ulrich persuaded everyone of the worth of 'Sandman', and in retrospect, he was dead right. That's not to say that 'Holier Than Thou' isn't a good track however because it certainly is, and if anything it's the closest thing on the album to the band's thrash metal roots.

The one feature of *Metallica* that set it apart from anything else the band had ever attempted was the slower songs, of which 'The Unforgiven' is the first. Fading in with what sounds like a horn and a guitar intro straight out of the Wild West, its peculiar arrangement surprises by possessing a heavy verse, leading to a mellow chorus (whereas it's usually the other way around). Hetfield's harmonies are nothing short of startling however, and the tense lyrical content somehow feels confessional. Old school fans of the band would initially recoil in horror, but the radio stations would love the new direction.

'Wherever I May Roam' is next, and in many ways it has a large, film-score type feel to it, with its distinctly Eastern guitar signature, and vague lyrics about endless time spent on the road. Hetfield's carries the road-dog vocals off brilliantly as you'd expect, and the track has been a live favourite ever since its release. 'Don't Tread On Me' is one of the record's weaker moments, with its lyrical origins referencing an American military force who carry a flag bearing the words 'Liberty or Death', along with a rattlesnake symbol similar to the one on the album's front cover. It's nothing complicated musically however, and plods along at a fairly pedestrian pace.

If there is true filler on *Metallica*, then track seven 'Through The Never' is surely it. While it's entirely possible that this innocuous track only appears so in the face of the rather stiff competition, it's neither particularly heavy nor groundbreaking, but thankfully, at four or so minutes, it doesn't outstay its welcome.

Now for 'Nothing Else Matters'. If there was ever a track that introduced Metallica to a completely new audience, it was this, a heart-on-sleeve, out-and-out ballad. Reputedly another Hetfield confessional about missing loved ones (girlfriends specifically), it was touching, and in one fell swoop a turning point in Hetfield's creative and (arguably) personal life.

In interviews, he himself admits that he stumbled on the simple open-string strum by accident, and that he initially felt very uncomfortable about sharing it with the rest of the band. The song was something that just could not be omitted. Vocally he's utterly reborn on this track, displaying a depth of touching harmony that nobody, perhaps even himself you'd suspect, thought he possessed. As if that wasn't enough, the blistering guitar solo that he delivers

– wrought with sheer emotion – is one of his best of all-time.

Anthrax's Charlie Benante was one peer who was blown away by Hetfield's performance: "I always thought of James as an exceptional guitar player and I always felt that when James played guitar it was as if he was expressing his emotions through the notes, as much as he was through his vocals. To me, I wish James played more leads, because his leads are incredibly emotional and different, and I can totally tell that it's him." Benante also had an opinion on Hetfield's new-found vocal harmony: "James wasn't originally what you'd classify as a rock singer, but as time went on people just adapted to that being his style and he became a singer."

After the melancholy splendour of 'Nothing Else Matters', the next track 'Of Wolf And Man' is relatively uncomplicated, both in style and of lyric. Its hunting theme (from the eyes of the hunter) is quite arresting, and Hetfield revels in delivering it with customary menace, particularly given that game-hunting was an interest he himself was developing.

Hetfield's views on faith and medicine are the subject on the gargantuan 'The God That Failed'; most clearly his thoughts on the effectiveness of faith, or rather its futility in his eyes. His mother's death from cancer when he was young must surely have been at the forefront of Hetfield's mind when writing this one.

Jason Newsted's first full writing credit comes in the form of the ninth number called 'My Friend Of Misery'. Apparently, Newsted was under the impression that his deliberate bass intro that begins the song was going to be spun-out to form a full instrumental, like those on previous albums. Hetfield had other ideas though, and the song ends up being essentially a very mid-paced, but nevertheless atmospheric hard rock song – a style that the band would sadly develop further in future years. Album closer 'The Struggle Within' is a short, sharp and relatively heavy track, featuring a sludgy main riff and some angry Hetfield vocals, all leading to an interesting multi-layered chorus.

Not surprisingly, the general reception from the critics was a combination of initial surprise at the wild change in direction, but ultimate satisfaction with the end product. Certainly, on purely a production level it was by far the best Metallica had ever sounded; a fact that's of great credit to Bob Rock and his vision for where the band were capable of going. So in that sense it became the benchmark for how metal albums should sound from that point on.

However, while other bands could maybe imitate *Metallica*'s sound, they just couldn't mirror the staggering song-writing abilities of Hetfield and Ulrich, and for that reason, Metallica stayed several large steps ahead of the metal pack. Not just that, with an album so approachable, they'd taken large strides to capturing a significant chunk of commercial listenership – a place previously occupied by the Bon Jovis, the U2s and the REMs of the world.

Entirely in keeping with its new place among such household names, *Metallica* ploughed headlong into the *Billboard* Charts like the juggernaut in the 'Enter Sandman' video, and for four consecutive weeks it sat at Number 1, proudly surveying its newly conquered kingdom – unheard of for a supposed extreme metal act.

The mainstream music press loved it – mainly because it was something they could relate to, but also because it was an album that they thought they could comfortably discuss with their readership. *Rolling Stone* magazine said: "Several songs seemed destined to become hard rock classics. They've successfully bridged the gap between commercial metal and the much harder thrash of Slayer, Anthrax and Megadeth." The UK's Q magazine was equally praising, and perhaps summed it up even better. "[It] transformed them from cult metal heroes into global superstars ... bringing a little refinement to their undoubted power." Pretty much everyone in print – from metal to men's lifestyle – recognised *Metallica* for what it was: a landmark in modern music – no band of this kind has come remotely close to replicating its impact to date.

Consequently, with an utterly monstrous album on their hands, Metallica were under pressure to deliver the goods on tour, and just as they had with ... *And Justice For All,* they hit the road before the album's actual release date. In keeping with their tireless and highly attentive touring habits to date, the 'Wherever I May Roam' tour did just that, and scoured everywhere you could think of – and a few places you probably couldn't too.

Kicking off in the band's home state of California at the little known Phoenix Theatre in Petaluma on July 1, the tour and its successor (appropriately named 'Nowhere Else to Roam'), would keep the band on the road for the best part of a staggering three years – surely one of the most intense tour schedules in rock history.

Shortly afterwards, the band once again took their enormous stage show to Europe, playing a show on Ulrich's childhood doorstep at the Gentofte Stadium in Copenhagen. A quick stop in Poland brought Metallica back to the now familiar scene of the 'Monsters Of Rock' festival at Castle Donington, where the band dominated a bill that included Mötley Crüe, AC/DC and erstwhile touring pals Queensryche.

Another significant show took place at an airfield in Moscow, where Pantera were also on the bill. Rex Brown and Pantera had been in the studio at the time, but didn't realise the significance the 'Black' album would have for them in the future. "It was us, The Black Crowes, Metallica and AC/DC," Brown remembers. "All I can remember is a sea of people, you couldn't count how many, and they all had flags of different countries. I remember that all James had for a backstage changing room was a tent!

Anyway, when we got back we were laying down drum tracks for *Vulgar Display Of Power*, and then 'Enter Sandman' dropped," Brown continues. "Then we heard the rest of the record, and we said, 'Okay, we are going to make a heavier record every fuckin' time we go out.' That was the only way we felt we could top ourselves, Metallica gave us a spot to do that in, because they were all over the fuckin' radio with this thing, and they could have easily been shot dead because of it."

With radio going mad for their album, the band rattled off a series of killer shows in the US that now incorporated their famous 'snake-pit' set-up, where guests of the band and privileged fans got to view the gig from a vantage point that was a sunken pit almost in the stage area.

Bob Nalbandian was there at one of the five nights the band played the LA Forum on that tour. "I was there with the guys from Armored Saint and I was sitting in the low section, and with the in-the-round set-up James was sometimes fifty feet way. I remember the lights came on the audience, and I was sitting with my buddies when James looked right at me and shouted 'Get off your ass!' and started laughing."

After that show, Nalbandian headed backstage. "A guy taps me on the shoulder and it was James who looked at me and said, 'When I tell you to get off your ass, I mean get off your ass!' I was amazed he recognised me and James said, 'Sure, I knew it was you', and we started talking about the old days."

October 12 saw the band roll back into Oakland for the 'Day On The Green' show again, on this occasion, with support from Faith No More and Queensryche. In short, it was something of a triumphant homecoming, complete with a similarly frenzied atmosphere to that memorable day back in 1985. Eric Braverman was there of course: "That was one of the most kick-ass shows in the history of metal right there," Braverman claims.

Chris Akin, one of the hosts of the *Classic Metal Show* – an excellent metal radio with bases in Ohio and Indiana – was also there. "It was awesome, any time you fence off the infield and turn it into a giant mosh-pit – there's nothing wrong with that!" Akin remembers, clearly referring to the Oakland Coliseum's baseball background.

The remainder of 1991 and 1992 were taken up with the huge touring commitments that the band had necessitated by crafting an album that the music public just couldn't get enough of. Notable events along the way included an appearance at Wembley Stadium for the Freddie Mercury Tribute Concert on April 20 (the band had previously successfully covered Queen's 'Stone Cold Crazy'), the release of the stirring 'Nothing Else Matters' as a single in May of that year, and some US tour dates with mega-selling Guns N' Roses, who themselves were riding high on their double album *Use Your Illusion I* and *II* – released together near the end of the previous year.

At that time, Guns N' Roses and Metallica were by far the biggest heavy bands on the planet, so to put the two together on the same bill was a potentially massive commercial draw. The bands paths had already crossed, at least on a social level, as both were hanging out in LA finishing albums, which inevitably led to all manner of drunken antics. Although Guns N' Roses often drew negative headlines for their debauched behaviour, according to Lars Ulrich the Metallica boys were every bit as bad.

Sadly, the shows together did not entirely go as planned. It seems that the sheer scale of operations, and the reality of being part of what was an increasingly 'corporate' set-up caused significant issues within the G N' R camp. That was problem enough, but when James walked into an exploding pyrotechnic during a show at Montreal's Olympic Stadium on August 8, Metallica had a bigger issue on their hands, and one far more damaging than Axl Rose's almost nightly headlines. James's predicament actually could have been a lot more serious but as it was, he suffered serious burns to his left hand and arm.

Obviously, the show stopped while James was given emergency treatment, and the confused crowd waited for the performance of Guns N' Roses. Bizarrely, Axl then announced that he had throat problems that meant he couldn't perform, an announcement that sent the crowd, who were already frustrated at Metallica's unfortunately truncated show, into a frenzy of anger.

Thousands of dollars of damage later, the Olympic Stadium was cleared, after what could only be described as a riot. As he had in 1986, John Marshall stepped into Hetfield's rhythm role for the shows that began on August 25 – two weeks after the incident. To mark the significance of that near-miss, Hetfield added a tattoo to that burned left arm that depicted flames, cards and the words 'Carpe Diem Baby'.

Finally, when the tour reached Seattle's mammoth Kingdome on October 6, 1992, the two biggest bands in rock parted company, seemingly on good terms despite what had gone on in Montreal. Metallica rolled into Europe thereafter, during which time two video tapes were released, entitled *A Year And A Half In The Life Of Metallica Parts 1* and *2*. Essentially documenting the making of *Metallica*, these tapes were of a significantly higher production standard than the band's *Cliff 'Em All* outing, and intentionally so. These two releases also featured footage from the early part of the 'Wherever I May Roam' tour that would officially come to a breathless and exhausted end in December of 1992 with some final European dates.

One of those dates threw up an interesting meeting between

Megadeth's bass player David Ellefson and Hetfield, as David himself explains: "They were on the 'Black' album tour and we were touring *Countdown To Extinction*. We ended up somewhere in Eastern Europe, maybe Budapest, and I hung out with James after the show. I grew up hunting and with guns, and that subject was our common ground that we chatted about. James told me about hunting wild boar, and while the obvious thing would be to talk about music, I always find common ground on a more human level."

You would have thought that Mustaine's Megadeth in company with Metallica would probably be an incendiary combination, but according to Ellefson, controversial matters didn't come up: "There was that connection, but I never wanted to go there, knowing it could have been a touchy subject. And also, it was not my issue to ever talk about, so I avoided it."

1993 began much like 1992 ended, with more exhaustive touring beginning in North America before another long trek to Australia and the Far East. On returning from there, the band played some more European gigs, most notably at the Milton Keynes Bowl on June 5, with support surprisingly from Megadeth. The event seemed to pass off without remarkable incident however.

Meanwhile for James and the band, the tour ground on through Europe, eventually emitting its final death rattle in the middle of July 1993. Given the vast amount of time the band had been on the road, you'd have expected Hetfield to disappear for months. On the contrary, he and Ulrich invested the next two months assembling a live package documenting the gargantuan trek that they had just finished. Metallica remained relentless.

Entitled *Live Shit: Binge and Purge*, this souvenir/collector's edition included both audio and DVD footage of three shows from various points in the tour. The audio was recorded in Mexico City in 1993, while the video concert footage was filmed in San Diego in 1991 and Seattle in 1989. Despite being an expensive item, the pack sold well when it was made available in November 1993, and Hetfield himself even spoke up about its rather hefty price tag: "If we put these things out separately over the years it would cost the same amount of money."

Regardless of the content – which was impressive given the inclusion of booklets, backstage passes etc – the price-tag of more than $80 for the most basic version was still quite steep, but it would serve to satisfy fan's needs for new material given how long ago *Metallica* had been released. Not just that, it would act as nourishment during the long time until the band released anything genuinely new. Metallica then hit the road again for a quick spin around North America on a jaunt called 'The Shit Hits The Sheds: Binging and Purging Across The USA'. After this brief outing, Hetfield and Metallica retreated to the studio for an extended period of time, and 1995 would conveniently represent the mid-point of the band's astonishing musical career to date.

After the almost unbelievable success of *Metallica,* and the huge tours that supported it, the band would take stock of the situation and evaluate their worth in an industry that was always changing. As mentioned, the grunge movement had swept the US and crept into other continents too, causing untold damage to some genres of heavy metal. Although the worst of that 'epidemic' was over, and Kurt Cobain, the most identifiable figure of the entire movement, was tragically already dead, the damage inflicted on the rock industry was to be telling. The onset of grunge had meant that many thrash bands were driven underground, or had to radically alter their sound to find an audience. Now that the boot was on the other foot, the backlash against grunge which began in the mid-1990s meant that something new had to replace it, as well as filling the gaping holes that had been wrought in the metal industry as a result of its success. As with most gaping holes, there is usually something on hand to fill it, and in this case that job would fall to Pantera, as Rex Brown explains. "Metallica had gone and made the big rock record, and you had grunge and all that, so there was this big fuckin' empty space there. We just happened to be the guys with the songs, and the perseverance to be the band to fill the gap with that grass-roots fuckin' sound."

Brown was right on the money, and while Metallica mixed in different and more commercial circles during much of the 1990s, Pantera were one band who kept gritty, thrash-orientated metal fires burning brightly.

Chapter 11

Cruise Control

If Metallica had never released another record after 1991's earth-stopping 'Black' album, their career legacy would be none the worse for it. Indeed, many hard-core fans would have been even happy to call it quits after ... *And Justice For All*. For some critics and fans, the band that Metallica became – and indeed the individuals they also became post-1991 – simply cannot be compared to that lean, hungry outfit that spat and bit its way out of the metal underground back in the 1980s.

Trips across America by U-Haul truck were replaced by blasts around the country by private jet, and it would be difficult to suggest that that kind of privilege and availability of resource doesn't have some effect on a person. As much as anyone who's publicly successful in any media capacity tries to retain a semblance of normality, the scale of the beast you have created almost makes that impossible on a day-to-day basis.

As far as assessing where James Hetfield was by the mid-1990s, we need to remind ourselves firstly where he came from, and secondly the tough nature of that ascent. The Hetfield of the early days in his musical progression seemed to almost thrive on the adversity of it all, and continually be urged on by a desire to escape the bland normality of Downey. His upbringing and family situation merely offered more reason to better himself, and it would only be once the blur of the really successful years had passed that he would have any time whatsoever to focus on himself the person. Those days had not arrived by this time though, these were the days where the hard work was done, and the band could take their collective feet off the gas and coast.

On a personal level, it must also be extremely hard to detach oneself from the stage persona one projects, and be merely the actual person you are – an issue which Hetfield of all people must have found extremely challenging. When you factor-in the suggestion that the stage presence was frequently fuelled by alcohol during this period, you have an understandably complex state of mind to unravel. The life of a high profile rock star simply isn't the same as a normal lifestyle, and many struggle to adjust.

As a general observation, there does seem to be considerable truth in the idea that wealth and success changes how you relate to people. "When you've got fifteen thousand people yelling at you every night," opines Eric Braverman, "and all the weird stuff that goes with being in one of these bands, you are not a regular person. It's almost impossible to get a real insight into the kind of life James Hetfield has because almost all the perspectives are totally skewed, and therefore not readily relatable to normal people."

There should be no doubt that life in a mega-selling rock band would not be as straightforward as you would think, and to be in what you'd imagine to be a completely secure financial position at a relatively young age would inevitably alter your perspectives somewhat.

What seems certain is that on a personal level, the barriers that James naturally put up as a young musician had not come down to any great degree. If anything, the intrusion of media and fans may well have added to a general distrust of some people. Similarly, his desire to control everything around him – a habit intrinsically linked to a defensive facade – were as strong, maybe stronger than ever. This is a part of what makes him a genius.

Anthrax's Charlie Benante has an opinion on the subject too: "Most of the time, people who are in this rock 'n' roll business almost feel like they have to put on a show even when they are off-stage," Benante offers. "And that becomes increasingly hard to do, because at least when you are on-stage you have a guitar or whatever in front of you, and you can easily portray that image up there. But once you are off-stage and people continue to believe that you are that person, I think that's when life becomes a challenge."

If life was a challenge for James, it didn't always show, and in

February 1995, he and Lars appeared as guests with Kirk Hammett on the KNAC metal FM radio station in LA. The station had been around for several decades, catering for various genres – although the 1980s and 1990s had very much been geared towards heavy metal. Sadly the station was having to close down, and that guest DJ slot on February 15 was the last show, so rather fittingly the last song ever played on KNAC FM was Metallica's 'Fade To Black', which Hetfield himself introduced.

Later that month, the band, Bob Rock and Randy Staub went to Plant Studios in Sausalito, California, to begin work on Metallica's sixth studio album that would become known simply as *Load*.

As the spring of 1995 wore on, it became apparent that the band were in a rich vein of creativity, and that there was significantly more material than would be used for one album. Whether it was the fact that the studio placement allowed more family access, or whether long periods on the road had provided new inspiration – who knows. Either way, everything on the surface seemed to be going well, and with the seemingly settled production team of Hetfield, Ulrich and Rock able to do little wrong, the future for Metallica looked very bright indeed.

Proceedings were so well advanced that the band actually escaped (literally) for some live shows called the 'Escape From The Studio' tour, which kicked off on August 23 at the now demolished London Astoria. That venue, compared to some of the places the band had played during the previous three years was quite literally like Metallica playing in your front room. Available only to fan-club members (the author included), Metallica ripped through a feral set which rates as highly as any in their entire live history. Even Hetfield himself – who at that time was sporting a bizarre mullet haircut – has mentioned in the past the amazing atmosphere in that sweaty hall, and the airing of two new songs '2 x 4' and 'Devil's Dance' was just swallowed up in a frenzy of band-love that night.

After that short 'surfacing for air', the band disappeared into the studio again, only emerging with any great intent in December where the honoured Motörhead's Lemmy by playing at his 50th birthday celebrations at the Whisky in LA, on December 14.

JAMES HETFIELD

The early part of 1996 was all quiet on the Metallica front: however for James Hetfield it was a difficult time. His father, whom he had gradually seen more of after an at times rather distant upbringing, had been suffering from cancer, and as a result sadly passed away early that year. In a moving interview with the band's official fanzine *So What*, Hetfield spoke very highly of his late father, saying that it was only later that he realised the large part his dad had played in his life and how much influence he had had on the young future Metallica singer. When they became closer friends later in life, Hetfield said he realised they had similar interests, and when his father became ill he admired his strength. And while admitting to battling with the ideology of Christian Science as a teenager and in his twenties, Hetfield went on to say that he realised how "magical and powerful" the faith was in his father's mind during his fight against cancer.

The previous April, Lars Ulrich had indicated that the album was progressing, and that some of the lyrical content may surprise listeners with its deeply introspective nature. Hetfield's open discussion with *So What* about his father's passing should have given some clue as to his inward-looking demeanour, and when he also talked about his frustration with religion in a way he hadn't before, it became obvious what Ulrich could be pointing towards.

It seems – given Hetfield's admission – that instead of slamming the door in the face of religion when his mother died and he moved to Brea with David, the concepts and principles of Christian Science actually stayed with him. While he may not have actively participated in its doctrines, it wasn't completely dismissed – which is a hugely surprising fact.

When you consider what James was actually doing during the period he described as 'his twenties' i.e. the LA club circuit, the move to San Francisco, New York and *Kill 'Em All* etc, it's astounding to now know that through all of that, religion was perhaps something he still gave more than the occasional thought to.

That information is fascinating, particularly when you consider the distinctly rebellious attitude Hetfield generally exhibited outwardly, and also when you notice his use of the word 'battling', which itself suggests that religion was much closer to the surface than was ever suspected.

Consequently, you'd suspect that Hetfield's emotional state while recording *Load* was considerably more receptive to feelings of regret or nostalgia regarding his childhood and early adult life. It would remain to be seen whether this more delicate state of being would manifest itself in his lyric and song-writing, or whether *Load* could even come close to replicating the unworldly impact of the 'Black' album on commercial terms. Fans and critics would not have long to wait however, as it was announced that Metallica's studio album number six would be released on June 3, 1996.

Before embarking on the task of appraising Hetfield and his band's musical legacy of the 1995-1997 era, it's important to make one fact perfectly clear: despite any claims to the contrary, there is little doubt that regardless of how Hetfield felt emotionally, the key influences which drove the albums *Load*, and its successor, were all his.

Yes, the band were given more input – mostly on a lyrical level – but the genres of music that spawned the thirty or so tracks that would appear over the next two years, had perhaps more to do with Hetfield, and maybe less to do with Ulrich, Newsted and Hammett. Hetfield had always been a country music fan, and an admirer of elements of the accompanying lifestyle. You need only look at his hobbies: hunting, motorbikes and drag racing etc, to know that the way he lived life was much more in keeping with that demographic, compared to the more cultured European mind-set that Ulrich favoured. It should perhaps come as no surprise then that the material that the band came up with at this point in their career should have his life ethos branded deep into its core.

What the press did not expect during the promo tour which preceded the release was the band's rather bizarre new look. 'Fashion' had never been high on the agenda for Metallica, and Hetfield particularly seemed to revel in his distinctly unkempt and hirsute appearance, reminiscent of a young Ted Nugent. To see him now with short black hair and wearing pinstripe suit trousers in the press shots was nothing short of a shocker. The rest of the band were no less different from how we'd come to know them –

sporting various attires complete with some degree of facial make-up, and in Hammett's case, an odd-looking lip ring.

Press and fans had no idea what to make of the new image, and it seemed astounding to many that the band who wrote songs like 'Damage Inc' or 'Battery' could ever be seen dressed up like this, but the band members themselves seemed unconcerned as to what anyone thought. The press shots in question were taken by revered Dutch photographer Anton Corbijn of U2 and Depeche Mode photographic fame.

The fact that Corbijn was in effect a fashion photographer said rather a lot about where Metallica thought they stood in the world in 1996, and it definitely seemed that their egos had (perhaps inevitably) been massaged thoroughly by the huge adulation their fame had brought them. This would all be okay of course, if the music still stood up to scrutiny.

Before a single note of *Load* was even heard, Hetfield was conspicuously quick to defend the new look as he told the Metallica website, www.metallicaworld.co.uk: "People freak out about things that are different. Five years [since the release of *Metallica*] is a long time. Nirvana came and went. A lot of things happened in that five years."

What was also surfacing during the *Load* sessions was an apparent shift towards bad temper on Hetfield's behalf as Lars Ulrich told *Rolling Stone* magazine: "The other day, we were talking about some song title, and there was something that didn't make sense. We were standing in the kitchen at the studio. I'm going, 'What does this mean?' And he goes, 'Fuck all this. I don't know what the fuck this all means. Jesus Christ!' Bark, bark, bark! Then he storms out of the room and leaves the studio. I'm just standing there laughing."

The release of the frankly weird first single 'Until It Sleeps' on May 20 did nothing whatsoever to allay the fears of the band's hardcore following. Creeping in almost apologetically with an insipid Newsted fretless bass accent, the song builds steadily into a perfectly standard radio rock tune – except that Hetfield's usually aggressive vocal delivery carries absolutely no threat whatsoever. Reputedly a song about James's father's recent battle with cancer, it certainly sent alarm bells ringing with its overtly 'soft' tones, and fans of the old Metallica could well have headed for the exits – figuratively speaking – without waiting to hear the rest of *Load*.

A listening party for metal fans was held on the May 28 at the Dynamo Festival in Holland, whereby the entire album was aired through the public address to extremely mixed responses, and a week later the controversial cover of *Load* made its worldwide appearance on record store shelves. Featuring a cover image entitled 'Blood And Semen', by New York-born photographer Andres Serrano, whose challenging work often uses bodily fluids as a medium.

Load's cover also featured a new and softer Metallica logo. While Serrano's garish artwork and Corbijn's camp liner photos of the band in make-up were not for those of a squeamish disposition, the fourteen songs that made up the overly fleshy seventy-nine minutes of *Load* certainly were.

'Ain't My Bitch' kicks things off and is by no means as bad as it gets, in fact if this mid-tempo riff-driven track had appeared somewhere later on the 'Black' album, nobody would have batted an eyelid. What it did possess however, was more of a groove-type feel or even a biker-rock type arrangement. In contrast to the dire 'Until It Sleeps', Hetfield's vocals are as gritty as ever and his pronunciation of the word 'bitch-aaah', is actually very amusingly memorable. Having said all that, it's hardly 'Fight Fire With Fire', and while one of the record's few highlights, its stomping, red-neck sound would set more alarm bells ringing for die-hards.

'2 x 4' wanders in next like a drunk off the street, and sounds tedious beyond adequate description. Based on a one-dimensional, lumbering riff, it's surely a solid contender (one of several on the album) for one of Metallica's worst ever recordings. Even Hammett's wah-wah riffing can't save the dirge, which seems to have zero in the way of lyrical meaning either.

Of similar tedium is track three, 'The House That Jack Built', which apart from going precisely nowhere, features nothing in the way of Metallica's strengths. It's all spooky sonics and weird Hetfield growls; simply awful. 'Until It Sleeps' has been discussed already, then only slightly more palatable – largely due to a Hetfield vocal delivery which is at least half-way convincing – is track five, entitled 'King Nothing'. Starting with a mildly sinister bass intro which leads to a riff that could be an extremely impoverished cousin of 'Enter Sandman', 'King Nothing' is a Hetfield rant about thwarted ambition, delivered by a band running with the choke all the way out in figurative terms. Originally called 'Mouldy' because the riff had apparently been around for years, 'Hero Of The Day' is bland enough to suggest it had in fact been decomposing somewhere. A clean intro and a pop-rock verse structure does nothing to enhance the song's insipid banality, and at the halfway point in the album, Metallica are – to this author at least – a band in deep, deep trouble.

Next track 'Bleeding Me' – originally suggested to be a Hetfield song about his father's losing battle with cancer – is actually one of *Load*'s best tracks. But only if the listener is willing to suspend knowledge of everything they have ever known about the band Metallica, and view this eight-minute plus epic in complete isolation. A lazy bass intro introduces Hetfield's soulful vocal, which as he told *Playboy* some years later is actually about alcohol and his battle with it: "Around the time of *Load*, I felt I wanted to stop drinking ..." Hetfield explained. "There's a lot of things that scare you when you're growing up; you don't know why. The song 'Bleeding Me' is about that: I was trying to bleed out all the bad, get the evil out." The song builds quite satisfyingly thereafter, to a refreshingly angry climax – restoring some kind of faith in the overall package. Hetfield's genius resurfaces, albeit momentarily.

Sadly, it was to be a false dawn, because 'Cure' is just a run of the mill blues-rock song about unspecified sicknesses and cures. Possibly referring to how people use alcohol, or indeed religion as an antidote for their individual 'illnesses', this cumbersome track simply fails to convince on either a musical or lyrical level. 'Poor Twisted Me' is another tedious slab of biker-rock based around more of Hetfield's introspective lyrics. Musically it's desperate stuff, with all manner of slide and reverb guitar effects that do nothing to salvage the wreckage.

Inspired by a conversation Hetfield had with country singer Waylon Jennings, 'Wasting My Hate' is at least a little more up-tempo. Beginning with weird Hetfield vocals which actually sound more like the White Stripes than anything else, it builds to a steady mid-tempo crunch while never approaching what you'd call genuinely heavy, or for that matter innovative.

The most controversial track on *Load* is without doubt the country ballad called 'Mama Said', which for many fans would signal the abrupt end of their relationship with Metallica. To the author's ears however it's a touchingly poignant ode to Hetfield's mother, and as such it should be taken precisely for what it is. Vocally, it's a strong and convincing performance, and while the very thought of Hetfield delivering such a delicate message is initially jarring, it actually works very well. For radio audiences it represented another acceptable Metallica incarnation.

Hetfield explained in detail how the song evolved, on the website www.metallicaworld.co.uk, saying it was written on an electric guitar initially and was not intended for anyone else to hear. He pointed out the country tinges and admitted that he was heavily into that style of music at the time. "I guess people were taken by the openness of it," he suggested.

Malcolm Dome defends Hetfield's position: "I think he took on the mantle that Cliff had, which is the person who wasn't just the metal-head, but was prepared to listen to country, Southern rock – lots of different kinds of music. And I think he's had that input on some of the band's better years."

'Thorn Within' and 'Ronnie', which follows it, are both awful but for different reasons. The former seems so unimaginative it's hard to believe it's a Metallica song, although Jason Newsted was reputedly heard to say it was his favourite track on the album. Where the aforementioned 'The House That Jack Built' is strongly vying for the dubious honour of the band's worst ever recording, 'Ronnie' is head and shoulders above any such challengers for that accolade. In fact it positively sneers at any suggestion that anything more profoundly mediocre exists within the entire mighty Metallica canon. A bluesy, tedious plod telling the story of some country boy going on a shooting spree.

Of only mild consolation is the lengthy closer, 'The Outlaw Torn': a sprawling epic not unlike the superior 'Bleeding Me' earlier. Hilariously, during the build up to *Load*'s release, Lars Ulrich actually had the confidence to suggest that this was greatest heavy metal song ever written. As decent as it is, it isn't even the best track on the album.

Despite *Load* being by far the least invigorating collection of songs that Metallica had ever assembled, the music press in general hailed it as a success, and like its infinitely superior predecessor it spent four weeks at No 1 on the *Billboard* Chart. *Entertainment Weekly* said: "[The album] captures the band's earnest pursuit of its Sisyphean mission: to create hard rock that reaches grown-ups and basement-dwelling teens." *The New York Times* saw it as a success too: "On *Load*, Metallica has altered its music, learning new skills. Hetfield has committed himself to melodies, carrying tunes where he used to bark, and he no longer sounds sheepish when he sings quietly." *Melody Maker*, the now-defunct UK weekly perhaps captured the feeling best: "A Metallica album is traditionally an exhausting event. It should rock you to exhaustion, leave you brutalised and drained. This one is no exception. It is, however, the first Metallica album to make me wonder at any point, 'What the fuck was that?' It's as if the jackboot grinding the human face were to take occasional breaks for a pedicure."

Although *Load* was initially well received despite its relatively lightweight pretensions, few could argue that it simply did not sound like a 'proper' Metallica album. The band themselves were well aware of that fact, and Hetfield even took time to defend it in an interview he gave to the press in Australia: "I really hope that they [the fans] can understand what we are up to. I hope that they can follow through with us." These comments clearly suggested that Hetfield was well aware that both the band's image and new direction were going to divide the fans, and they even hinted that Hetfield felt that *Load*'s loose style had maybe even taken things just a little too far.

There's little doubt that on a stylistic level, *Load* was a reactionary album to some of the more rigid arrangements that they'd been bound to previously – particularly on *... And Justice For All*. The thing was, if they'd made this super-loose, biker-rock album immediately after *... And Justice For All*, it may well have been a major career-threatening issue. But because of the enormous commercial success of *Metallica*, the band basically had created themselves a license to go wherever they wanted in a musical sense, and this detour was the result. In a nutshell, they had 'bought' themselves their freedom, and they'd make full use of that luxury in future years.

Author Joel McIver – while not a huge fan of the album's actual music – understands what the band were attempting. "I think they tried a few different directions with the honest intention of exploring new territory, but those ideas simply didn't work."

Testament's Chuck Billy was another who was far from convinced by *Load*, particularly from a James Hetfield perspective, as he explains: "The whole band got to contribute on the *Load* record, and at that point I decided that James had to sing his own lyrics [for the best results]. When you sing your own lyrics, you sing them with more conviction and belief. When I heard that record it sounded to me like it wasn't him ... and it wasn't the James that I knew. There were none of the clever lyrics and clever parts and it changed how I felt about their music."

Rex Brown of Pantera was someone who actually benefitted from Metallica's deviation, and he didn't give *Load* a second thought. "All that make-up and shit? I really didn't know what to think. I didn't even care because by that time we were headlining arenas. It wasn't the brand of shit we were doing, and we kind of took over that spot where they left off."

As far as seeing James and the band around at the scene at that time, Brown is a little bemused about the circles Metallica were running in. "We only saw them spasmodically, but when we did, Lars would come in with fuckin' John McEnroe! You know, it was crazy. I don't think James was hanging out with all these artsy fuckin' dudes though. He's not that kind of guy."

Despite resistance from a few camps, by anyone else's standards, *Load's* sales figures (to date it has sold in excess of five million copies in the US alone) would represent colossal life-changing success, but for Metallica it was a mere sideways step – hardly a surprise given the untouchable precedent the 'Black' record had set. What was of bigger concern was the confusing musical conundrum posed by *Load*, and how it could be followed. Was thrash gone forever? Was this new look here to stay?

Well, only time would tell, but in the meantime, the band did what they know best, and went out on tour. Two fan club shows got the ball rolling on June 23 and 24, followed by a spot on the summer Lollapalooza tour which that year featured Soundgarden,

Rancid and The Ramones among others.

With one grunge act and two punk outfits in the upper echelons of the line-up, some questioned Metallica's role in such a non-metal collection, and a few added that fact to *Load*'s non-metal pretences and came up with the conclusion that Metallica had deserted their metal roots permanently. However, Hetfield jumped to his band's defence when quizzed on their exact motives: "We did Lollapalooza because we wanted to and it was cool. It was as simple as that. We got to see a few great bands and make some new friends. We played in front of some people who came to see us and some who wouldn't normally listen to us."

Although Lollapalooza was a success, it was more significant in that for its duration, Jason Newsted travelled separately from his band-mates – a fact that was indicative of some festering differences of opinion between Hetfield and Newsted. Indeed, although *Load* had been more of a band effort in some ways, Newsted himself actually had no writing credits whatsoever on it; a scenario that certainly raised a few eyebrows given his ten-year long tenure. This issue of freedom to create might not have amounted to much in 1996, but as time went on it would become a bigger problem as Hetfield increasingly tightened his grip on the band's extra-curricular activities.

Departure to Europe for the irritatingly titled 'Poor Touring Me' jaunt through now established cities, and the release of the horribly poppy 'Hero Of the Day' as a single, took up most of late September. Unsurprisingly, this new radio-friendly Metallica sound was lapped up by mainstream audiences, resulting in a Number 17 pitch on the UK charts. More autumn dates in the UK and Europe brought the band back to London to appear on the *Later With Jools Holland* TV show where Hetfield performed a rather nervous version of 'Mama Said', while the band joined him for versions of 'Wasting My Hate' and 'King Nothing'.

A video featuring Hetfield wearing a cowboy hat while sitting in the back of a taxi strumming a guitar accompanied the release of 'Mama Said' as a single on November 18. Although it was a new look for the man, it was one which he carried off rather well; certainly more so than the awkward dapper image that heralded the album release.

Again, and because of a mainstream audience's identification with a mellower Metallica sound, the single did well, reaching Number 19 in Britain, and doing similarly well in other markets overseas too. Touring continued throughout the end of 1996, and into the first half of 1997, with the brief interruption of Lars Ulrich's marriage to Skylar Satinstein. Hetfield performed 'Best Man' duties, although the whole event was only acknowledged the following night at the American Music Awards where the band received an award for 'Best Metal/Hard Rock Album'.

Romance was not only limited to Ulrich however, and Hetfield himself was in a steady relationship with long-term girlfriend Francesca Tomasi – a one time member of the band's behind-the-scenes team. When the tour finished in May, the band had a couple of spare months during which time Hetfield tied the knot with Francesca on August 17.

As discussed previously, the *Load* sessions had been reputedly a very productive time in the studio – with way too many tracks recorded than could fit on one studio album. Since this author contends that the already over-long *Load* wasn't actually very good at all, the thought that there was more material that *didn't* make the cut, was indeed a worrying proposition. After Hetfield's wedding and some festival dates in Europe, it was announced that a follow-up to *Load* would be released in November, consisting of more songs from the same recording sessions.

"We wrote 27 songs for *Load* and were developing it as a double album," Lars explained to *Billboard* magazine. "We then got the offer [in January 1996] to play Lollapalooza [that summer] and [decided] we [would] put one record out now with most of the songs that are done and then we [would] come back after a year and finish the rest of them. As far as I'm concerned, you can take any of these songs and interchange them on the two albums. The only fear we had was getting to it quick. We didn't want to leave it lying around for three years and worry about what it would sound like when we came back to it."

A month or so prior to the new album's release, Metallica performed two acoustic sets at an event organised by Neil Young to raise funds for the Bridge School for disabled children in San

Francisco. It was appropriate that Young should be the organiser, as in many ways he shared some similarities with Hetfield on a musical level. Additionally, 'Mama Said' wasn't exactly a million miles away from the kind of stuff Young specialised in. The same applied to 'Low Man's Lyric', a new track the band aired, which had almost a blue-grass feel to it. The band was also joined on-stage by Jerry Cantrell of Alice In Chains, when they covered Lynyrd Skynyrd's hangdog anthem 'Tuesday's Gone'.

Cantrell has always had a strong affinity with Hetfield's qualities, as he explains: "James is top of the heap to me. He always has been. I admire the way that he chooses to live and his fingerprint is absolutely all over the band and its music." It was reputedly an energetic evening with other performances from Lou Reed, Smashing Pumpkins and Alanis Morissette to name a few, and the event would subsequently become an important annual fixture.

For Metallica fans, any excitement they may have had was tempered somewhat by the release of the first single off the new record, entitled 'The Memory Remains'. Anyone who hoped *Load* had been but a mid-career wobble and that the band would get back on track, would be bitterly disappointed when they heard it. Not only is the song rather boring, it also features an odd cameo from Marianne Faithfull – a collaboration that could only strike bemusement into the psyches of true fans. It did sell however – reaching Number 13 in the UK – while laughing in the face of critics of the new direction at the same time.

If anything, this new track was somewhat worse than most of what *Load* had thrown up, and the weird collaboration merely highlighted the song's lack of imagination. Two free shows, one at a parking lot in Philadelphia, and another at a London dance venue called Ministry Of Sound, ushered in the release of *Load*'s sequel entitled *Reload*.

"It's the second half of *Load*," Ulrich told *Metal Edge* magazine. "Only it's coming out a year and a half later." What was rather revealing was that along with *Reload*'s release, which incidentally coincided with that of Celine Dion's 'Let's Talk About Love', Elektra also planned an advertising campaign on Comedy Central's rather crude show *South Park*.

While undoubtedly a shrewd move to get the message out there about a new album, it also said a lot about what the label considered the general age of Metallica's listenership to be. There was little doubt that since the 'Black' album, the average age of a Metallica fan had become progressively younger. Combine huge commercial outreach with *Load*'s laid-back, if rather weak alternative appeal – and that appearance on the Lollapalooza tour – and the reason is plain to see.

Sadly, no amount of advertisement, gimmickry or defence from the band themselves could alter the fact that *Reload* was nothing more than *Load*'s poor relation. Given how deeply unsatisfactory *Load* was, the suggestion that its successor was significantly worse was really saying something. When the record eventually did hit stores on November 17, 1997, many people questioned the timing of another release, particularly given that Metallica had historically taken their time between albums.

Hetfield's response to the questions was understandably defensive: "We liked the songs, and we wanted to get back into the studio after less of a tour. A lot of them needed a little work ... and I think at the end of the day, it's us pleasing ourselves. We're selfish bastards, and have been since day one, and that's how we've stayed pure and how we've kind of lasted all this time."

'A little work' indeed. 'Fuel' is the start, and by no means the album's worst moment. At the very least, it makes up for what it lacks in lyrical integrity with some degree of pedal-to-the-floor speed. Not speed in the sense of old Metallica of course, this is much more generic, but velocity that was welcome in the face of *Load*'s generally crawling tempo at least. The lyrical content, while simplistic, gives a clear indication that it's another Hetfield-inspired theme, drawing a simplistic comparison between a car's engine and a human body's need for fuel. He does at least deliver it with considerable conviction too – the only time he would do so on *Reload* actually.

'The Memory Remains' as described previously, is sheer agony, and 'Devil's Dance' which follows is probably worse. Both are lumbering, tedious pieces, which despite Hetfield's best efforts to create a feeling of sinister foreboding, both fall on their swords. As a reprise to the 'Black' album's stunning 'The Unforgiven', track four 'The Unforgiven II' is a misguided attempt to revisit a classic

– and apparently its very existence was a significant catalyst in the decision to release *Reload*.

"We thought, 'Let's continue a story and make part two of a song we've done before,'" Hetfield told *Billboard* magazine. "The whole aura of the music felt like this could really be a nice way to continue the story on 'The Unforgiven'. It wasn't like I thought I was going to be an unfulfilled person until I continued the song." Sadly, the sequel fails to capture any of the drama of the original, and its tired verse and chorus structure – while similar to its predecessor – sounds oddly hackneyed here.

While the up-beat 'Better Than You' represents some kind of return to form, 'Slither' and 'Carpe Diem Baby' just lower the quality level again with benign riffs in both cases. 'Bad Seed' is a desperate affair too, with little to commend it musically and some tired biblically referenced lyrics.

Reload does have a couple of decent moments however, and 'Where The Wild Things Are' and 'Prince Charming' are certainly two of them. The former is like a father's words to his child, warning him/her of life's pitfalls, whereas the latter is an interestingly psychedelic jaunt about gratuitous wrong-doing (not an Adam And The Ants cover, alas).

'Low Man's Lyric' reveals more of Hetfield's Irish-folk hankerings, sounding a bit like how Thin Lizzy (of whom Hetfield was a fan) might have done if they had recorded this kind of material. Sung from the standpoint of a vagrant, it's perfectly acceptable but hardly inspiring.

The album closes with two more slabs of sheer mundanity in the straightforward form of 'Attitude', followed by the far too long and boring 'Fixxxer', by which time the author for one, is happy to see the end of another extremely disappointing collection of Metallica tracks. *Reload*'s cover continues its predecessor's fascination with body fluids, being another rather abstract Serrano image, but this time substituting urine for semen. Charming stuff for sure, but the effect the second time around was far less effective.

On balance, *Reload* is very similar to *Load*, therefore you have to question the rationale behind both releases, when surely one album containing the 'best' of both albums would have achieved the same end. Both are overly long anyway. This author's opinion of *Reload* was by no means the consensus; reviews of the album by the mainstream titles at least were extremely positive. *Rolling Stone* called it as they saw it, although their assessment that the music was, "Strongly rooted in the group's apocalyptic metal sound ..." was indeed a strange one. *Musician* was even more dramatic when it said, "greasy, driving, full of fat grooves, lyric and rhythmic hooks, and sonic curveballs ... [it] captures one of rock's greatest bands at its peak."

Both magazines were perhaps overstating matters, but what those reviews did indicate was that Metallica's audience had become considerably more mainstream since 1991, and the fact that a relatively conservative music press was praising the material suggested that a huge climate change had taken place. In all honesty, *Load* and *Reload* are as good, or as bad as each other. Despite the negativity in some metal quarters, *Reload* did go on to sell almost five million copies in the US and occupy the Number 1 spot on the *Billboard* chart.

Brian Slagel – a long term ally of the band – was someone who appreciated the *Load* and *Reload* eras, as he confirms: "The band was listening to a lot of 1970s metal at the time, so the albums were influenced by that stuff, and not the NWOBHM stuff they had been influenced by before. I really like *Load* a lot and think there are some great songs on it. Also, Bob Rock had more influence on them as he was more into the rock 'n' roll stuff."

"Personally I think *Load* and *Reload* had some really good moments," Malcolm Dome suggests, providing some balance to the Metallica mid-career debate. Eric Braverman isn't a fan of the whole era however and Jason Newsted himself said in one article that he was uncomfortable with the photographs and artwork – although he qualified that by saying he later grew to like the cover art as a "positive" sentiment using the two life forces of blood and semen. "The band was totally out of touch with their fans," is Braverman's less encouraging opinion. This personal view actually poses an interesting question: who exactly *were* Metallica's fans in 1997?

The fact of the matter is that the fan-base was actually in serious transition – something which had probably been happening since the 'Black' album catapulted the band into the living rooms of the world in 1991. While some die-hard thrash fans from the early days would hang on and hope for a return to the heavy stuff (the author included), others had no doubt deserted the band years ago for harder alternatives. While that erosion took place, a whole new demographic of Metallica fans would climb on board. You could therefore argue that the sound of *Load* and *Reload* was probably perfect for their tastes – disproving at least part of the theory that the band had detached from their fan-base at the time.

While the two albums certainly were a departure, and the product of a freedom already discussed, they were a reflection of where the band were at that juncture, and consequently attracted an appropriate listenership. After all, both albums sold serious units, which in itself says a lot about the band's cross-spectrum appeal during the late 1990s.

Chapter 12

Back To The Garage

While the *Load* and *Reload* saga represented transition for Metallica and their millions of fans old and new, the period was also a pivotal time in James Hetfield's life. His father's death, followed soon afterwards by the happier news of his own marriage must surely have combined to put him in a new emotional place, and this was obvious in his creative output during these few years.

While it's certain that these two records are far from Metallica's best, they both offer clear views into Hetfield's soul in that they allowed him to play the kind of music that he *personally* enjoyed – with no need to fear the consequences on any level.

Country, blues and Southern rock have always been key components in Hetfield's make-up, therefore at some point in his career their influence was always going to come out. So it might as well have been at the point in his career where a negative response was least potentially damaging. Throw in the fact that by doing so, Hetfield had also attracted a new type of fan, and you can draw a line under the era as a pretty notable success (unless of course you were a fan of thrash metal – a genre that was undergoing a battering at this late 1990s juncture).

1998 began with another Metallica wedding – this time Kirk Hammett's – who tied the knot in Hawaii with his girlfriend Lani Grutadauro. For the band, the release of the weak but popular 'Unforgiven II' on March 3 heralded the beginning of another stint of intense touring activity, with the 'Poor Touring Me' production dragging its ass to Australia in April. James Hetfield had other fantastic developments going on in his life too, with the birth of his first daughter named Cali Tee Hetfield who arrived on June 11, 1998. Hetfield flew back to California during a gap in the tour, and was present at his daughter's birth.

After only two weeks at home, James was needed on the road again for the US leg of the tour which swung through America's East Coast en-route to Texas. With sold-out shows and enthusiastic responses to the new songs played live, it seemed that despite the radical change in musical direction, Metallica still commanded huge box-office attention. 'Fuel' was released as a single on July 4 before the tour came to a pause in San Diego in the middle of September.

It wasn't to be a period of rest however, as the band went directly into the studio to record some cover versions which would later appear on an album called *Garage Inc.* The release of this new material was promoted with a series of small club shows with a Metallica tribute band called rather appropriately Battery, and when the record did appear it would be marketed as a double-album with the first side featuring the newly recorded covers, and the second side showcasing much of what had surfaced on the earlier *Garage Days Re-Revisited* EP, plus some extra B-sides.

Of the new material, versions of tracks by Diamond Head ('It's Electric'), Black Sabbath ('Sabbra Cadabra') and Mercyful Fate (a medley including 'Satan's Fall', 'Curse Of The Pharaohs', 'A Corpse Without A Soul', 'Into The Coven' and 'Evil') were fairly logical tunes to re-work. Less obvious were versions of Nick Cave's 'Loverman', Bob Seger's 'Turn The Page' and Thin Lizzy's 'Whisky In The Jar', although the latter at least fitted in with Hetfield's obvious high regard for Phil Lynott's poetic lyrical abilities. Released on November 23, *Garage Inc.* landed as either a two-CD set, or three vinyl long players, with a cover image featuring the band members looking like four grease-monkeys at a local auto-shop.

Lars Ulrich for one was keen to point out how much more relaxed this album process had been compared to previous studio excursions: "It's definitely easier to work with other people's material," he said in an article called 'Garage Days' on www.metallicaworld.co.uk: "We like to turn them into something very Metallica, different than how the original artist did it. You don't get so fucking anal about it, and you can bang these covers out in like five minutes."

The critical response to what was effectively an intriguing stop-gap was very positive, with most recognising that the band were keen to identify their broad slew of influences. From a sales perspective, you could hardly complain either as *Garage Inc.* would ultimately go on to sell in excess of five million copies – not bad for a covers collection.

Rolling Stone said, "Gloriously hard as the album is, you can't miss Metallica's good-natured side coming through." *Entertainment Weekly* felt similarly, when they said, "We'll have to wait until Metallica's next 'proper' album to find out if this trip to the garage recharges their batteries. Still, all things considered, *Garage Inc.* is an intermittently exhilarating joyride."

Not content with the airing of a covers album, the band also put out a live DVD package on the same day called *Cunning Stunts,* including an unusually dull live performance of the band playing a show on the *Load* tour at Fort Worth, Texas in May of 1997. Featuring a broad spread of material from across the eras, this DVD fell relatively flat in the eyes of more than a few fans.

The awards kept coming in early 1999 with the band bagging another Grammy in the category of 'Best Metal Performance' for one of *Reload*'s brighter moments, 'Better Than You'. Metallica's cover of Thin Lizzy's timeless 'Whiskey In The Jar' was also released as a single, and like most of the band's offerings, made a minor impact on the UK charts reaching Number 29.

Shortly afterwards the band was honoured at the Recording Industry Association Of America show, with their selection for a much coveted Diamond Award in recognition of 10 million sales of *Metallica*. It got better too, when April 7, 1999 was officially declared 'Metallica Day' in San Francisco – an amazing coup for any act, far less a heavy metal behemoth like Metallica.

April of 1999 also threw up a new direction for the band, and one whose roots lay in an orchestral score of the 'Black' album's 'Nothing Else Matters' by composer Michael Kamen. While the band actually resisted putting in too much of Kamen's orchestral arrangement on the song back in 1991, there had also been another rendition nicknamed 'The Elevator Version' – featuring much more of Kamen's lavish orchestration. Seemingly, around that time, Michael Kamen had made a throw-away remark to Hetfield about the possibility of him arranging and composing a full concert, combining Metallica with a full-blown orchestra.

While the response was positive, and the band really liked what Kamen had done with the alternate version of 'Nothing Else Matters', some considerable time had passed and the idea had, in Kamen's mind at least, seemed shelved. Not so, apparently, as Kamen received a phone call from Q Prime's Peter Mensch saying words to the effect of "Metallica will do that concert you talked about." Kamen was seemingly astounded that the idea was even still under consideration, but equally enthused by the fact that the band wanted to take him up on it.

This wasn't a completely new concept for Kamen though, as he'd already had orchestral dalliances with giants of popular music like Deep Purple and Eric Clapton, but there is little doubt that in terms of sheer ambition, a venture of this kind with Metallica would certainly eclipse all of that.

The plan was to marry up Metallica with the San Francisco Symphony Orchestra, with a view to releasing a double live album and accompanying DVD entitled *S&M*. Hetfield himself told *Rolling Stone* magazine how the project came about. "Maestro Kamen came to us with the idea almost two years ago. He had done projects with other rock people, like David Bowie, Eric Clapton and Pink Floyd. He wanted to get a little more extreme, so he chose us. I'm sure there's something more extreme – he could have picked, like Graveworm – but I think we were a pretty good choice. We said, 'Hell, yeah'. You don't pass these things up. It took two years to pull together – from the initial idea to deciding which orchestra to picking the songs."

The band were still involved with what was called the 'Poor Re-Touring Me' jaunt, with support from Monster Magnet, but two dates on April 21 and 22 were set aside to record with the orchestra at the Berkeley Community Theatre. The two shows were recorded before the band took off for Mexico and South America, prior to swinging back up through Europe with added back-up from Mercyful Fate and Apocalyptica. The latter were something of a one-off band, being a Finnish act composed of classically trained cellists, with their own unique take on some Metallica tracks.

European commitments wore on until July, when the band

returned to New York State to perform at the Woodstock show with nu-metal mega-sellers Limp Bizkit, among others. Metallica's set was marred by considerable violence – a feature of that year's event as a whole – and instead of being a celebration of a famous musical gathering, Woodstock 1999 was little more than a bad tempered riot.

November 23, 1999 saw the release of *S&M* and the rock world held its breath, given that this was the kind of ambitious move that could go one of two ways. The band promoted the album release by doing two similar shows accompanied by orchestras, firstly in Berlin, and later in New York City.

The primary concern was not the fact that an orchestra was involved (this was an entirely acceptable addition as far as most metal fans were concerned); it was more of an issue to see if the orchestral arrangement could actually complement Metallica's diverse set. In many ways, some classical composers were playing their equivalent of heavy metal for their era, so the two genres are far less detached than might initially seem the case.

What was different about the making of *S&M* was the fact that on a production level, the record was crunched out very rapidly – by Metallica's standards at least. While Bob Rock was still behind the controls, his input would have necessarily been less than on standard studio records, and Kamen's arrangements would have dictated matters significantly. Both are credited on the sleeve notes.

The live show *S&M* begins with Metallica's now familiar intro, Ennio Morricone's 'Ecstasy of Gold', and immediately the benefits of a large orchestra are blatantly apparent. Where the traditional taped show intro sounded tinny and almost clichéd, this new incarnation sounds majestic, and the perfect precursor to such a dramatic amalgam of worlds. 'The Call of Ktulu', with Hetfield's mesmeric, clean intro benefits similarly, and all of a sudden any doubters of the project were questioning what they ever had to worry about.

The skill of Kamen's arrangement was that of co-operation between the two parts of the show, and so far that was the factor which made it work. Sadly, things go a little wrong on 'Master Of Puppets'. Maybe it came too early in the set, or possibly it was just that the track is much too complex. Either way, the band and the orchestra do little other than battle each other throughout, rendering this live version far inferior to its studio original. 'Of Wolf And Man' from the 'Black' album follows, and while not an obvious selection, it actually works out well.

'The Thing That Should Not Be' is another less obvious live choice but all concerned had clearly done their homework, because it's super-heavy riff is beefed up hugely by the orchestra. Worth noting is Hetfield's vocal faux-pas where he actually misses a line and starts laughing. Generally though it's another high point; unlike Reload's 'Fuel' and 'The Memory Remains' – both of which benefit minimally from exposure to this re-work.

Perhaps S&M's best moment is the first of two new tracks written specifically for the album, 'No Leaf Clover'. While closely linked in style to much of the *Load* and *Reload* era material, it is far more catchy and memorable – benefitting hugely from the monstrous assistance this arena offers. It also features a curiously mainstream Hetfield vocal style, one which other band members – particularly Jason Newsted – had doubts about, according to the S&M documentary. It's probably the album's best moment, and it's a shame the song hadn't surfaced in the studio previously. 'Hero Of The Day', 'Devil's Dance' and 'Bleeding Me' which come next are all adequate renditions of the originals, as the first half of the album draws to a close.

'Nothing Else Matters' begins the second half, and while you'd expect this track to work best given Kamen's earlier exposure to it, on the night the song actually sounds less convincing than the original, largely due to an annoyingly nasal Hetfield vocal style which actually detracts from the melody. 'For Whom The Bell Tolls' however, is a different story. Its tempo and style are ideal for this type of collaboration, and of the older material, this one sounds by far the most invigorated.

The second new track, 'Human', simply doesn't work at this level, and its laid-back stoner rock riff gives the orchestra little to feed off. The vast sprawl of 'Wherever I May Roam' restores order quickly, followed by the epic vista of 'Outlaw Torn', whose ten-minute bulk is improved significantly by some atmospheric orchestration, not to mention some great reverbed Hetfield vocals.

The S&M experience is brought to a close with four integral

parts of the band's back catalogue, and by and large they all work well – largely due to the fact that they are undeniably great songs that would stand-up anywhere. Of the four, 'Sad But True' is the weakest, whereas 'One', 'Enter Sandman' and 'Battery' sound passably loyal to the originals. The problem with *S&M* was one of consistency, which meant that the band was always recovering from a weak moment or falling flat from a strong one. On some occasions, the marriage of band and orchestra simply did not sync. However, fans of the band were enthusiastic, and Metallica themselves certainly enjoyed the experience. It would also be notable in that *S&M* was the last album that Jason Newsted would appear on.

As with most of Metallica's output to date, the response of the music press was supportive, with many recognising the ambitious nature of the project and tailoring their review accordingly. *Rolling Stone* went over the top, while only offering a moderate score, when they said the record, "creates the most crowded, ceiling-rattling basement rec room in rock … [in its] sheer awesomeness … the performance succeeds … the monster numbers benefit from supersizing. The effect is … one of timelessness."

Britain's Q magazine was a little more cautious however, suggesting, "another just about forgivable flirtation with Spinal Tap-esque lunacy … a fine hit-heavy live LP with bolted-on bombast from the S.F. Symphony … Michael Kamen's scores swoop and soar with impressive portent throughout."

In some ways, *S&M* had successfully restored some fans' faith in the band after the confusion of *Load* and *Reload*. But not everyone was convinced. "*S&M* was a misguided thing," suggests Malcolm Dome. "It was an interesting idea, but I don't really think that the band and the orchestra connected, apart from on the new songs. Otherwise, it was a band playing the songs the way they know how, with the orchestra having to fit-in where they could."

Sales *were* good however, and with the band on a high at the end of 1999, they powered towards the Millennium on the M2K tour accompanied by Kid Rock and Sevendust. The year culminated in Detroit with a show supported by Ted Nugent, which became known as the 'Whiplash Bash'. Metallica were still on top of the pile.

The new century was obviously a huge opportunity for rebirth and development for everyone involved, but for Metallica, the year 2000 was to be nothing but problematic. Having just about survived the 1990s with their credibility intact, they were about to be put in a position that would test the loyalty of their huge fan-base to the absolute limit. Bizarrely, it wouldn't be the actual music the band produced that would cause the problem, but more the way that the music was being used and distributed.

During early 2000, Metallica recorded the single 'I Disappear', an average tune in all truth which was intended to appear on the soundtrack to the block-buster movie *Mission: Impossible 2*. February saw the release of the excellent live version of 'No Leaf Clover' as a single as well as the band collecting another Grammy for 'Whiskey In The Jar'. Of more concern was the fact that bootleg versions of 'I Disappear' had been heard on various radio stations, and this was some months before the actual soundtrack was due for general release. Not only that, the version that appeared was not in fact the version which was due to appear on the movie's accompanying album. The source of the material turned out to be the internet, where songs in file form could now be easily shared and distributed among like-minded users.

One of the main exponents of this file-sharing phenomenon was a site called Napster, which allowed users to register and search for free music files online. The potential implications for the music industry were beyond huge, simply because this process completely by-passed the conventional sales structure and the music in effect became a freely available commodity. Obviously, a band like Metallica saw this threat as just too big. Consequently, in April of 2000 the band took legal action against Napster and three other collaborating American universities, with the main thrust of the action based on the infringement of the band's copyright.

What followed over the next few months was a gargantuan legal battle, with Lars Ulrich championing the Metallica cause against Napster, and not the 300,000 users who'd been identified as having downloaded free Metallica songs. It's unnecessary to document the full minutiae of the case here (Hetfield's role in it all was very much back-seat), but it's worth mentioning that he was supportive of the action.

His only comment at the time was that, "We are going after Napster, the main artery. We are not going after the individual fans." Clearly this was an attempt to appease the hordes, but at the same time it was a comment intended to make it clear that he and his band would not tolerate such perceived infringement of their rights.

Ulrich held-off furious fans with a whip and a chair in May, who oddly felt betrayed by their heroes for not letting them download their music for free. What some fans missed however was the fact that Ulrich was completely entitled to defend his and his band's creative output, given that file-sharing was actually illegal. James was at home with his family following the birth of his second child, Castor Virgil Hetfield. He was probably quite happy to be out of the limelight at this stage, although Ulrich's popularity as the band's spokesman was declining, and that of Metallica would worryingly soon follow.

There was touring business to undertake too, so in June the band took off on what was called 'The Summer Sanitarium' tour, which must have been a source of great relief given the negative and unjustified fan uproar that had been flying their way. Kicking off the through the East Coast states, the tour proved eventful and tragic, with the death of a fan who fell from an upper balcony at a show in Baltimore, Maryland. Hetfield was in the wars too, injuring some discs in his back which resulted in him missing three shows in early July. Help came this time in the form of an amalgam of artists like Korn, System Of A Down and Kid Rock, who between them performed some Metallica songs as an interim measure.

The tour continued with Hetfield returned to full fitness, but in the background the Napster issue loomed large. Early August signaled the end of the tour and for James Hetfield his public business with the band for that year was largely done.

In a *Playboy* interview in 2001, Hetfield explained his feelings about Lars taking charge of the war against Napster. "My wife and I were giving birth to a second child. And family is *number one*. So Lars had to run with the torch, and there were a few bad moves. You know, Lars can get really mouthy and be a snotty-nosed kid at times. I cringed at certain interviews: 'Oh dude, don't say that.'"

The year 2000 ended with the Napster issue unresolved, as well as several other lawsuits the band had taken out in the interim – for example, against a perfume company for calling one of their products Metallica. Why any company would call a product such a name is amusing, but Metallica were understandably less amused. The year was over, and they had survived it – just about. Yet while Napster would rumble on, there were intra-band issues that would pose more immediate problems … and they had been bubbling under the surface for some time.

Chapter 13

Playboy

The New Year began dramatically for Metallica fans, with the shock announcement in mid-January that Jason Newsted was quitting the band. The main reason Newsted initially gave was that he was risking causing his body actual physical harm by continuing. That reason was perfectly plausible too, particularly as Newsted had had continuing back problems – his explosive on-stage style was certainly physically very demanding. However, there was a strong feeling that this was just one factor in his decision to quit, and plenty of observers conjectured about a possible continuing breakdown in communication with James Hetfield.

When Jason joined the band, Eric Braverman – his close friend – had queried what would happen if and when Jason stood up to Hetfield. While there had been occasional rumblings of discontent, as well as the continuing absence of much in the way of direct Newsted writing credits, it had never really come to a head. The reason it had now was possibly more to do with Newsted's decision to be more vocal, rather than any particular elevation or change in Hetfield's status. Hetfield it seemed, was just being Hetfield ...

While it was obvious that he wasn't exactly thrilled by the whole Metallica environment, it would only come out sometime later that much of Newsted's frustration hinged around Hetfield's intolerance of any extra-Metallica projects (despite having done a few himself over the years – Hetfield had appeared on some Corrosion Of Conformity albums and a couple of other projects, but to be fair these had always been low-key and he had not promoted his involvement in any way). Newsted had become part of a side-project called Echobrain – a pop-rock act who sounded nothing whatsoever like Metallica.

While Metallica had intimated that they would be heading into the studio 'sometime soon', it appears that Newsted was not keen to sit around in the meantime and do nothing, so he threw himself with good faith into the Echobrain project without even considering that it would become an issue.

For Hetfield however, it *was* an issue – so much so that he was willing to say it was not acceptable for band members to do their own thing outside of Metallica itself. At the time of Newsted's departure, however, this information was slow to emerge and on the surface it just looked as if the natural time for Newsted to move on had arrived. The official biography on the band's website states, "No one reason can be fairly the cause, more several long-standing issues that silently grew beyond their initial molehills."

In an interview with Joel McIver soon after his departure, Newsted seemed happy with his decision, if a little unclear and evasive about some of the more personal issues which came into the equation. When asked if it was solely an issue of looking after his body, Newsted threw in a few scraps that suggested there were other factors too. "I wasn't confident I could be the '110%' dude performer that people know me as, and I needed to have that. And now that I've had a year to think about it, I think that … James, where he was in his headspace, you know, at that time, with his personal life and different things."

Even from such a cryptic explanation, it was obvious Newsted still had great respect for Hetfield – and certainly recognised his importance in holding the whole Metallica deal together. It would be a while until the real story would come out, and until then, speculation ensued regarding the identity of Newsted's replacement in the band.

Joey Vera was a name that came up as a possible replacement – just as it had fourteen years earlier – and Newsted himself definitely felt that whoever replaced him needed to be not just a seasoned player, but also one who would be able to deal with the bigger Metallica issues comfortably. Vera certainly fitted that bill, at least in Newsted's opinion, and the fact that he was well known to Hetfield and Ulrich made him one of the more obvious choices. Not just that, Vera's own career with Armored Saint – while moderately successful by comparison – could never be likened to the success of the Metallica story, so it was an opportunity that may well have suited both parties in 2001. He wasn't the only choice though, and over the next few months, several bass player names were touted around, with no fixed choice being reached at that stage.

The Napster issue was an ongoing ordeal for Ulrich and the battery of legal representation Metallica had in place, but the battle was one that the band was winning, given that a court had agreed with certain key aspects of the Metallica case. While that task fell to Ulrich to orchestrate, James Hetfield remained relatively low-profile in the legal and press discussions.

Of more immediate significance however, was a major interview that appeared in the March 5 issue of *Playboy* magazine, where the band members – including the now departed Jason Newsted – parted with some of the more insightful pieces of information the public had ever been party to. It wasn't a conventional article either, as all four members had been interviewed separately, but the results were depressing for sure, and gave huge clues to suggest that not all had been good in the band for some time.

While Ulrich's interview largely focused on Napster and wider band issues, the other three took things down a more personal route, with Hammett particularly effusive about some of the more unpleasant aspects of his upbringing. From Hetfield's perspective, the most telling pieces of information were the references to his levels of alcohol consumption. "I had to have a bottle of vodka just for fun. I'm surprised I'm still alive," Hetfield told Ron Tannebaum, who was conducting the interview.

Newsted had something to say about Hetfield's drinking habits too. "James is the only one that ever drank so much that that he couldn't show up for a rehearsal or for photos," Newsted was reported to comment.

While Hetfield's drinking habits had always been well known, there was a sense that now they had perhaps become a bigger issue. It wasn't that James was unaware of that fact either, and he'd already attempted to address the matter himself by briefly seeking therapy during the *Load* era. "I took more than a year off from drinking – and the skies didn't part. It was just life, but less fun ...

The evil didn't come out. I wasn't laughing, wasn't having a good time. I realised drinking is a part of me. Now I know how far to go." Later in the article he said, "I wouldn't say that I'm an alcoholic – but then you know, alcoholics never say they're alcoholics."

While none of this was particularly new information – at least for people close to the band – when the subject turned to Newsted and intra-band anxiety, Hetfield's sense of humour quickly disappeared. Hetfield's view was that he couldn't relate to why anyone would want to do anything outside of Metallica firstly, but he also felt that to do so would actively detract from what Metallica were all about. Newsted would have said all he had done was to entertain himself creatively while his primary concern Metallica was on a break between albums. Newsted had apparently argued his case vehemently regarding Echobrain, and repeatedly made his view known that the side-project could in no way compromise his involvement with Metallica. In *Playboy* he stated very clearly that, "I would not leave Metallica for another band. If I ever happened to choose that path, I would do it to live my life, not depart to play in another band."

Hetfield just did not see it that way however. In the same *Playboy* interview, Hammett said, "James demands loyalty and unity, and I respect that ..." Hammett also told *Playboy*, "I think it's morally wrong to keep someone away from what keeps him happy."

Newsted had most to say however, and it was clear that he felt that Hetfield was being unfair. "James is on quite a few records: in the *South Park* movie, when Kenney goes to hell, James is singing, and he's on just about every Corrosion Of Conformity album," Newsted commented.

But what of Hetfield's position? It's easy to criticise and point the finger at the man, and to suggest that his view of extra-curricular activity is entirely to blame. What must be considered however is that *without Hetfield's strength of character*, and strong sense of unity, would Metallica have been the monstrously successful story that they became? He was the frontman and a key songwriter, but there was also a huge aura around his personality that undoubtedly boosted Metallica's profile.

After all, few would argue that in order to hold any entity

together, it generally requires a strong person at the head of affairs to deal with the vast array of personal dynamics that arise as a result of living and working in a massive rock band. Additionally, there's a need for an able communicator and 'face', and those were certainly two distinct roles that Hetfield and Ulrich had respectively gravitated towards.

Therefore, while both current and ex-band members might have had plenty to say about Hetfield's hard-line approach, there is absolutely no doubt that it was intrinsically vital to the survival of the band. It would be hard to say that his desire to influence every aspect of Metallica had ever been to the detriment of the band's incredible forward progress.

Time would tell, but in the meantime, the band tried to put a distinctly positive spin on events, as Hetfield commented in an interview at the ESPN 'Action Sports & Music Awards': "We're really enjoying each other's company and retouching on things we haven't connected on in a long time. It's a fun and healthy time for us."

It's uncertain exactly what the 'things' that Hetfield was referring to were, and although Ulrich mentioned (on the Metallica website) that the band felt no particular pressure on a musical level, he made no mention of this period being a particularly harmonious one.

For Ulrich, the pressures of the Napster issue clearly dominated his thoughts, and there's little doubt that the band had lost many fans as a result of it all – rightly or wrongly. Few would argue that the decision to sue Napster was the right approach – and one that definitely nipped the concept of file sharing in the bud for other acts in the future – but for their critics, it was the *way* that they did it that grated.

Whatever was going on with Napster, Metallica entered their recording space in San Francisco with Bob Rock to start recording some new material. The location of the studio was the Presidio – a former army barracks, and a significantly different environment from anywhere they had worked before. This was intentional of course, and a conscious effort to change from the comfortable studio environments of the past. It was also hoped that the results would be similarly uncomfortable.

Eric Braverman was familiar with the venue, and for him it gave some indication of how high the band was flying. "It's the most expensive real-estate in the world maybe, "Eric Braverman suggests. "They all have their own individual offices in there and shit."

Nothing was heard from the band until two months later, when it was announced that the war with Napster was essentially over, and that a compromise situation was reached out of court (the press release said, "The settlement will enable the parties to work together to make Napster a positive vehicle for artists and music enthusiasts alike."). Shortly afterwards, there was a vacation period, and Hetfield used that to embark on a bear hunting trip to Siberia. Hunting had always been high on James's list of recreational priorities, but this particular trip was considerably more remote and solitary than anything he'd previously undertaken. Bears were hunted obviously, but in addition, James spent a lot of the time holed-up drinking vodka – seemingly the only fluid readily available. During that period he also missed his son Castor's first birthday.

The next time any news came out of the Metallica camp was in July, and this time it was to announce that all album activities including recording had ceased, while James Hetfield entered rehabilitation to "undergo treatment for alcoholism and other addictions."

While the exact timing was certainly surprising, the facts of the announcement came as no shock, particularly given the fact that Hetfield's drink issues were already well documented. What was slightly more unnerving was the mention of "other addictions", and speculation was rife as to what they were. Of all the people to dispel the erroneous and hurtful rumours, Jason Newsted was the man, quickly dismissing any suggestion that James had any drugs issues. It says a lot about Hetfield's growth that he was willing and able to address his actual issues; to quit drinking would clearly benefit both his personal and business life. And he had, after all, always made it clear that family was number one.

The response to the news was generally positive, and messages of support flooded in from friends and peers across the industry.

There were dozens of people who were happy to come forward as admirers of the man – with little bad to say whatsoever. Fred Cotton was as close a friend as anyone, although he hadn't had much contact with James since the late 1980s. "It wasn't like anything happened between us or anything." Cotton says. "Our lives just went in different directions. I still love that dude like a brother though, even to this day."

A short time into the rehab period, a message appeared from James on the Metallica website: "It took a lot for me to admit to my problems, and it's a great feeling to have the support and comfort for me as a person from all the friends I've made out there. Thanks very much, it means a lot."

Understandably after that, little was heard from Hetfield for several months, until another message appeared from the website, which read: "Yes folks, we have word from James, and the news is all good. His recovery has gone exceedingly well; he is back out, about and feeling good about life." This was indeed good news, and Hetfield added his own message: "My music and lyrics have always been therapy for me. Without this God-given gift, I don't know where I'd be ..."

As a result of the *Some Kind Of Monster* documentary – for which initial filming had begun in the spring of 2001 (prior to Hetfield leaving), we now know that during Hetfield's days in the rehab wilderness, his band-mates wondered if he would ever actually return to Metallica. Lars Ulrich found this especially hard to take, and the concept of James not returning led to Ulrich's suggestion that Hetfield controlled when he was present, and controlled when he was absent.

Without the presence of James Hetfield, Metallica would surely not exist. Take Hetfield away? ... Therein lies a huge reason for why the man is so important. It's only when he wasn't there that the stark reality of his absence hit home, so the rehab period was as good a time to regroup for the others as it was for James himself. Put simply, James Hetfield is the beating heart of Metallica, and while the possibility of him never returning existed, there must surely have been a few anxious faces in the larger Metallica camp as the weeks became months in 2001.

As it turned out, they need not have worried; James Hetfield emerged from rehab on February 19, 2002, seemingly a reformed character. While James had been away, his wife Francesca had given birth to their third child, Marcella, who arrived on January 17. The prospect of another child in the family combined with a continuing desire to improve his mind-set must have been huge incentives to triumph during the arduous process of intensive rehab.

Unsurprisingly, when news of James's recovery broke, there was significant relief on all fronts – and intrigue as to exactly which James would return. Prior to Hetfield's hiatus, the band had been receiving counselling from a life coach called Dr Phil Towle – a guy more famous for dealing with large sports franchises.

On a general level, Towle's role was to facilitate improved communication and understanding between high profile, large earning individuals. While there was little doubt that Metallica had lost the ability to communicate, and that fact had certainly influenced their creative output, it was however, a concern to many observers that such an extreme 'therapy' type approach was necessary for a gnarly rock band. Jason Newsted certainly thought that the approach was overkill, and in an interview for *Some Kind Of Monster*, he described the situation famously as, "Fucking lame ... weak."

A brief appearance at the MTV *Icon* show, where Hetfield honoured his heroes Aerosmith, resulted in James's first venture on-stage since rehab, and he himself admitted he felt the pressure. "This is the first time I have been on a stage since I came out of rehab, so I'm a little nervous. My heart is pounding fast, so let me know if I am talking too fast."

Quite a shy and touching episode from Hetfield in many ways, and worlds away from the overconfidence most people exhibit while fuelled by alcohol. The signs for those who sought a more relaxed Hetfield were definitely good. Jason Newsted also reported positively, following his first post-rehab meeting with James. "He's a changed man ..." said Newsted. "It was good ... we're brothers, man."

2002 continued with little news of either new material, or the other small matter of who was going to play bass on the new record – an issue that had understandably become somewhat secondary. What seemed most likely was that producer Bob Rock would fill-in on bass duties, at least until a suitable replacement for Newsted could be identified. What was known was the band had moved, and would end up recording at their own studio space that was simply referred to as HQ. That process began in earnest on April 12, 2002.

While locked away in HQ with a recently re-habbed Hetfield, the discipline of recording an album had seemingly changed immeasurably since the last time in the studio. The simple reason for that was that as part of James's therapy, he was only willing to commit certain hours (11am until 4pm) each day, to work activities – a sensible approach, surely, given the context of his recovery. For Ulrich particularly, such a specific time contribution was a serious problem, especially given his renowned partiality for being nocturnal. Consequently, it meant that there was a huge conflict from the start.

The new informal agreement was that there should be a far more equal level of contribution from all band members – with all three taking equal hand in writing music and *lyrical* ideas. That would have been fine, but Hetfield's daily curfew meant that the situation simply did not always work out so well. One of the bigger ironies of this new working arrangement was that one of Jason Newsted's issues with the studio had been there wasn't enough individual input. Now, after he had left, this was happening.

Despite all these new working practices designed to gently break Hetfield back into life in the studio, very little was known about what kind of music the band was working on. What had come out was that it wouldn't be a polished affair, instead using rawness and spontaneity to reflect the various moods at the time. That sounded quite promising in principle, particularly given the hard rock feel of *Load* and *Reload*, and it was even suggested that the band would be revisiting the sound of their early material.

One theme that kept coming out of any discussion was 'anger', and as 2002 rolled into 2003, it would be fair to say that nobody outside of the band had any sort of clue as to what this new material was going to sound like. That confusion wasn't exactly helped by Kirk Hammett's mentioning of Swedish band

Meshuggah as a possible comparison either, and matters were only made worse when Ulrich added Hatebreed and Entombed to that list of influences (in retrospect, a combination of any of the above would have been welcome).

What definitely assisted matters – and finally helped the band's Presidio and HQ period turn the corner – was the announcement of Rob Trujillo as Metallica's new bass player. Trujillo was of Mexican descent, and had been plying his very able trade with Ozzy Osbourne's band, and prior to that, with hardcore/metal act Suicidal Tendencies. Footage of Trujillo being offered the role sees Metallica stress he is a *member*, not a hired musician and you can't help but admire the open way in which the three existing members welcome him into the fold.

Seemingly, the band had been astounded by how easily Trujillo managed to deliver the vast array of Metallica bass-lines he'd been asked to learn, and all who saw his first rehearsal agreed he was the man for the job. Crucially too, Trujillo was a quiet and extremely polite individual. Unfortunately, for Trujillo, his arrival was too late to facilitate any involvement on the new album; those bass parts had already been handled by Bob Rock for recording purposes.

As far as the album was concerned, there were increasing suggestions that it would sound raw and under-produced, with considerable influence drawn from the hard months the band had endured in order to arrive at its conception. Although he'd certainly borne the brunt of the unhappiness, James Hetfield seemingly saw things differently now, with ever more increased emphasis on the importance of family.

What that meant for Metallica would remain to be seen, but at least Hetfield recognised that his controlling habits were not a positive feature: "Lars and me came into the studio and told the others what to do …" Hetfield admitted. "Everything had to be under my control. Totally childish."

Gradually, a picture was building regarding the likely sound of the new record, which was to be called *St. Anger* – a concept loosely based on the St. Christopher pendant that many people wear for good luck. Producer Bob Rock – a master of polished, commercially appealing rock records – gave an interview with *Metal Hammer* and seemed liberated by the 'no rules' approach they had taken in the studio. "We wanted a raw, unpolished sound," Rock admitted. "We played it all live without overdubs ... for example I only needed ten minutes for the drum sound."

On the surface, all of that sounded promising of course. But given all that had gone on in the Metallica camp in recent years, there was definitely a sense of apprehension as to the likely quality of the results. The build up to the release continued at pace during the spring of 2003, with the band recording a video for the first single (the title track) at the infamously tough San Quentin prison in San Francisco. With a summer tour looming with support from nu-metal duo Limp Bizkit and Linkin Park, it was time to deliver *St. Anger* to the expectant masses.

The band had another duty to perform too, and that was to head to LA for the MTV *Icon* show, which that year would honour them. It was a strange night – particularly for Rob Trujillo – involving several mainstream acts (Avril Lavigne etc) doing their own take on a few Metallica tracks. It was very much a tribute on behalf of MTV, especially given that Metallica had hardly been 'their kind of band' for the bulk of their career. But if nothing else, it did offer some healthy publicity for the release of the new record.

So, with the customary frenzied media machine firmly in motion, the album was released on June 5, 2003. Interestingly, this was five days in advance of the planned release date but the decision was taken to go ahead early for fear, rather ironically, of a premature leak onto the internet.

Chapter 14

The Well Is Dry

The number thirteen is an unlucky one for many. With that in mind, it's entirely appropriate that a chapter involving Metallica's seventh full studio album *St. Anger* should carry that number. The suggestion that the album is one fuelled by sheer anger and misery is perhaps a little misguided however, and in some people's eyes (the author included), the record is not particularly angry at all – just very average.

From the very first seconds of lead track 'Frantic', there are serious issues with the general sound of the recording – despite the song itself being one of the better tracks on the album. There's a distinct feeling that the riff doesn't have any particular direction – the muddy sound doesn't help, and Hetfield's vocal delivery is acceptable without being truly arresting. As Metallica lead tracks go, it's weak, and the album suddenly has a lot to prove.

Thankfully, the title track is much better and possesses some similarity to the band's thrash metal roots. Hetfield's vocals are poor however, but as a composition it at least has a game plan – something that can't be said for track three, 'Some Kind Of Monster'. Apart from being a really infantile title (it was a joint effort as we later discovered in the documentary of the same name), it's a rather boring, down-tuned song, during which Ulrich's infuriating drum sound really starts to grate. A snare sound like banging a dustbin lid had never appeared before.

What was also different was that the rhythm guitar assault that had been so potent on early Metallica albums seemed to carry far less threat on this album. On closer inspection, Hetfield was playing single, more resonant power chords as opposed to fast, technical riffing, with the only speed in each song coming from Ulrich's often irritating drum-sound.

Aside from the sonic issues, what is also interesting is that during the process of recording *St. Anger*, Hetfield himself made several references to the fact that the lyrics and sound were influenced by the difficulties of the previous months. In actual fact, the lyrics on the album are some of the band's least insightful, and 'Dirty Window' is a prime example. A tedious, lumbering riff and laboured lyrics by Hetfield just aren't cutting it at all, and the hideous Ulrich drum sound is already threatening to render *St. Anger* unlistenable.

"Rarely have I seen such an error of judgement by a band. The way that *St. Anger* was written, recorded and performed was 100% wrong," rock writer Joel McIver reckons, and he may well have a point. Things get worse too. 'Invisible Kid', while surely intended to be a cathartic exercise for Hetfield, instead falls flat on every level. Dull lyrics, a boring riff and that awful, muddy sound again add nothing to what is already a misguided track. "I understand the mechanics of recovery," Joel McIver acknowledges, "but addiction is neither expressed or resolved with songs like 'Invisible Kid', which are dross of the highest order."

'My World' is marginally better however, albeit little more than a straight-ahead rock song. It does at least have some kind of direction. That said, the muddled vocal chorus is forgettable. At this point in proceedings most Metallica fans were surely despairing as to what had happened to their band, and many of them would have been happy to revisit *Load* and *Reload* in preference to what they had heard so far. 'Shoot Me Again' does nothing to restore the faith either. Although the quietly delivered verse sections are quite infectious, the chorus is almost cartoon Western stuff, and as such, the song just doesn't work.

'Sweet Amber' is one of the better moments, although that isn't actually saying a lot. A quiet, lilting intro moves into a riff that would actually be quite satisfying, if it wasn't for the fact that the muddled sound allows far too many moving parts. 'Unnamed Feeling' begins with a weird chugging intro and that Ulrich garbage can drumbeat. Hetfield then delivers a strange, indistinguishable series of sounds before the song begins in earnest. 'Purify' is at least mildly aggressive, but just like everything so far the ideas seem at best half-formed. Finally, and with some relief, *St. Anger* grinds to a halt with the acceptable nine-minute sprawl of 'All Within My Hands', a song perhaps about James's predilection to sometimes choke the life out of the band. The last section of the song is the only indication that there is any kind of anger going on at all and, as such, it's quite satisfying. Overall, it's depressingly predictable stuff though, and in the grand scheme of the Metallica back catalogue, it's a B-side at very best.

The general reception to *St. Anger* was mixed at best, although predictably – like most recent Metallica records – it occupied the top spot on the *Billboard* Chart, among many others. For many critics, *St. Anger* was just too much to take. Even the cover art felt unimaginative, featuring a tightly restrained fist on a cartoon orange background. While Malcolm Dome wasn't impressed, he managed to qualify his criticism somewhat: "*St. Anger* was an awful album for sure, but at least it was *their* awful album. By that I mean it wasn't a compromise of any kind, and was a statement of where the band was at that time."

Hugh Tanner, who'd spent years looking in on Hetfield's career as a friend and as a fan of the band, had a balanced view of what it represented for all involved. "In many ways, it was a raw record they had to make, in order to bring to an end a raw period in the [lives of the] individuals involved."

While there is truth in all the above comments, more critical commentators viewed the record's supposedly 'angry' nature to be a cover for a desperate lack of ideas and direction. The mainstream press were confused, but at the same time hesitant to completely rubbish what many believed to be an honestly delivered statement on where the band stood emotionally at the time. The garage-like sound was identified almost across the board, although the lack of coherent song structures was attributed – at least in some reviews – to Metallica going 'back to basics'.

Amazingly for an album that was supposedly an open forum for all members of the band, there were no guitar solos whatsoever – a fact that even Kirk Hammett had to try and justify. Apparently, it was an attempt to do what wasn't expected, and an urge to not conform to what was expected from a heavy metal band of their kind. What it ultimately turned out to be was a move away from the strengths of the band, and almost an exception in their largely strong back-catalogue.

Regardless of the lukewarm reception that met *St. Anger*, Metallica rolled its huge production out on a summer tour with Limp Bizkit, Linkin Park and the Deftones – drawing vast audiences all over the country. The year of 2003 involved the release of 'Frantic' as a single as well as the more significant news that the aforementioned *Some Kind Of Monster* movie was to be released to the public. As we already know, the movie was not a polished, feel-good exercise designed to extract more money from the fans; this was a raw, documentary-style piece, covering the entire *St. Anger* process from Jason's departure through to album release. Also included were interviews with the band while James went into rehab, discussions with therapist Dr Phil Towle, and various other chats with other members of the Metallica 'family'.

To achieve all that, the film was necessarily highly intrusive, and the intrusion would be carried out by a couple of talented filmmakers by the name of Joe Berlinger and Bruce Sinofsky. These characters were already skilled in the art of raw documentaries of this kind, and had actually approached the band some years earlier with the idea, only to be told that Metallica were not yet ready to bare all at that stage. Regardless of their worthy track record in honest, cutting-edge filmmaking, nothing could have prepared them for the drama of the Metallica monster.

Berlinger himself was keen to identify the thrust of the film when speaking to the media: "On the surface it's about the making of *St. Anger*, but it's much more a film about human relationships and the creative process." It certainly was, and the relationship that was placed under most scrutiny in the process was the one involving Hetfield and Ulrich. Without examining every detail of the film, it became fairly obvious that while the two thought they had been communicating over the years, the reality was perhaps somewhat different. Much like many marriages and other close relationships, too many assumptions are made, resulting in the gradual formation of a chasm of mis-understanding.

In Hetfield and Ulrich's case, Lars openly admitted to not knowing his colleague at all, and some of the documentary's scenes depicted palpable levels of tension between the two. It was however compelling viewing, and far more interesting than any reality TV show, with some added spice in the form of an interview with former band member Dave Mustaine. The key to the issue was that Mustaine felt disrespected because of what happened all those years ago in New York. He also seemed to feel that the whole issue could have been handled completely differently and the problems could have been averted. It made for compelling viewing.

Dr Phil Towle, whose role it was to identify key issues with the band's past, saw the Mustaine saga as one of great significance, and one which definitely needed resolving. Consequently, Mustaine came to San Francisco and was given the opportunity to talk on a one-to-one basis with Lars Ulrich – the main focus of his irritation over the years. While the painful conversation with Ulrich unfolded, Mustaine looked drained. Ulrich on the other hand, seemed sheepish talking about the past, and while mildly apologetic about it, seemed surprised by how hurt Mustaine seemed to be.

The one person missing was James Hetfield however – a fact identified by Mustaine himself – and while that was the case, no full closure was ever going to come. Hetfield had chosen to distance himself from the whole Mustaine debate over the preceding years in actual fact, preferring to keep his thoughts on the matter fairly quiet. Anytime he was pressed, he had always took a diplomatic stance, and avoided going down the road of actually disrespecting Mustaine. Despite the attention it got, the Mustaine issue was not the focus of the documentary. The main purpose was to re-establish connection between the existing band members, while at the same time revealing Hetfield, Ulrich and Hammett's true personality to the fans.

Joe Berlinger explained to the press how, "James views it as something which allows him to communicate with the fans, to let them know who he really is. It shows his whole psychological mission ... he could no longer pretend he was James Hetfield the frontman off-stage and on." Berlinger was right of course, although it's arguable whether the film itself illustrated the reason for James's going into rehab.

Whatever the actual why's and wherefores, *Some Kind Of Monster* was a huge turning point for Metallica as a band. Because it was so honest – almost painfully so at times – it unwittingly served to clear away all the myths and bullshit that had accrued over the years, giving the band a clean slate on both a professional and personal level. As you'd expect, Metallica fans flocked to see the movie, which aired in theatres worldwide in the middle part of 2004. Surprisingly, it wasn't a huge commercial success, and despite the human story involved, it barely crossed the line between a specialist release and a cross-spectrum blockbuster.

The band themselves were involved in touring at the time, having paused briefly to collect another Grammy award for 'St. Anger' in the 'Best Metal Performance' category. While *St. Anger* still sat rather uncomfortably and split the fans right down the middle on an approval level, the live Metallica experience continued to impress – a fact that has always been the case, even in troubled times. 'The Unnamed Feeling' surfaced as a single, making it the third off the album so far, although sales continued to be relatively poor by the band's previously gargantuan standards.

"During those so-called faltering times, every single live performance was beyond un-faltering," Eric Braverman protests. "The saddest thing about all of this, is that [people] thought that all the blame fell on James Hetfield. I mean, who wanted to hear him singing 'Mama Said'? Everyone of those shows on that *St. Anger* tour, James Hetfield delivered the shit. It's the albums that have been the problem, never the live show."

While James continued to deliver compelling live shows as if nothing had happened – a few people noticed that on a personal level, Hetfield was indeed a different proposition after rehab. Anthrax's Charlie Benante was one of them. "I hadn't seen them for a while, but we ended up playing together in Germany while Metallica were promoting *St. Anger*. I had the most down-to-earth conversation I had ever had with James on that trip. I had gone through some stuff during the years prior to that where I was having these anxiety attacks. As a result I had to stop drinking ... and in fact taking any stimulant. I had a bit of an awakening about things and we talked about that. He talked to me about what he went through and it was a very emotional talk. After that I would get text messages from him sporadically, and we would communicate that way."

Benante had known Hetfield since those early days in New York, and although they had drifted apart occasionally over the years, they were probably closer now than they had ever been. The reason for that – in Benante's opinion – was that James was now finally comfortable in his own skin. "I guess after I watched that movie, I kind of understood a little more," Benante muses. "And I guess what he was saying to me all made sense now."

Lonn Friend had his own problems in 2004, and was blown away by any meetings he had with the reformed Hetfield during the Californian leg of the *St. Anger* tour. "We had infrequent, but always warm visits over the years, most significantly around the time of the Metallica shows in November 2004," Friend recalls fondly. "The band had just emerged from their *Some Kind Of Monster* season in hell, but I was going through a divorce while living in the desert writing my book. James understood, and offered consoling words. It was a moment between semi-kindred spirits."

Frenetic touring, the release of the song 'Some Kind of Monster' as an EP, and no small amount of exhaustion brought Metallica back to San Francisco for Christmas of 2004 – drained emotionally by the rigours of live shows and the aftermath of the *Some Kind Of Monster* experience.

What they did say was that while they had been on the road, they had spent some time jamming on new material, and there seemed to be the considerable likelihood that the results of those sessions would surface in the near future. With a fresh dynamic operating with new bass player Rob Trujillo, Metallica had amazingly managed to negotiate the hardest times of their entire career to date. While the music had certainly suffered, the positives of a new-found respect for each other on a human level would certainly ensure a solid future.

For James Hetfield it was the beginning of a new life, and it wouldn't be overstating things to describe the whole rehab experience as his rebirth. He definitely viewed things through different eyes, and on a personal level that was a huge step forward. For the first time in his entire career he felt able to be just James Hetfield, with nothing to prove to anyone else, or indeed himself. What that would mean for his music and the wider trajectory of

Metallica, would remain to be seen. But without the experiences of the previous four years, it's entirely possible that Metallica would not be a functioning band.

Chapter 15

Man In The Box

By the end of 2004, it was being rumoured that Metallica had already assembled many hours of their customary riff ideas, song fragments and bass lines. It definitely seemed as if the fog of the preceding years had lifted, and for James Hetfield personally, this was certainly a new dawn. What would prove interesting however, was the question of whether the new Metallica – with a sober Hetfield – would be able to summon the kind of aggression and creativity that their extremely tolerant fan-base wanted.

There was little doubt that the whole process of self-analysis had taken a heavy toll, and combined with the usual punishing touring schedule, it would have been no surprise if the band had disappeared for much longer than they did.

Hetfield had already announced during a radio interview in 2004 that the band planned to begin work on new material during the spring of 2005. Nothing particularly came of that suggestion in public however, and 2005 was a quiet year on most fronts with the exception of another Grammy nomination for *Some Kind Of Monster* in the 'Best Hard Rock Performance' category.

There was one rather significant announcement that year however, and that was that Metallica had parted ways with producer Bob Rock. Although they had no plans as to who would produce future material, the band felt that the relationship with Rock had reached its natural conclusion.

"As grateful as we are for all Bob has done for us since 1991, we feel it's time to move on," Lars Ulrich said in the official press release. Hetfield threw in his own comments too: "We've been thinking about this for some time now, it's just the way things have panned out."

Other than that, the band did their own thing, with Kirk

Hammett taking some time out to perform with the FLUX string quartet. For James Hetfield, this was family time, and that was something he was truly relishing. Amusingly though, the band did get together in September for the purpose of recording their voices for the *Simpsons* TV show, on an episode which would go out sometime the following year. November of 2005 saw the band's only live shows of the year, and they didn't have to travel far – SBC Park in San Francisco being the venue for two concerts in the middle of the month.

The earlier suggestion that new material was imminent proved somewhat unlikely however, and a further announcement in early 2006 confirmed that very fact. In reality, it wouldn't be until March 2006 that Ulrich would announce the band planned to dedicate the next six months to a new album. While they were doing so, Metallica had some other commitments, one of them being to induct Black Sabbath into the Rock 'n' Roll Hall Of Fame in March. It was a stirring event by any standards, and featured respectful speeches from both Lars and James, as well as Metallica renditions of Sabbath classics 'Hole In The Sky' and 'Ironman'.

Additionally, the band had touring commitments that year, and that involved three shows in South Africa before they returned to Europe for the annual summer festival route, including the UK's Download Festival in June. After these shows, Metallica headed to the far East for end-of-summer gigs in Japan (where new material was aired) and South Korea. On the commercial front, it was a relatively quiet period, with only the release of an acoustic set from 1997 for the Bridge School Benefit, and a DVD of all the band's videos to date seeing the light of day in 2006.

It wouldn't be until early 2007 that Metallica would give clear signs that any new material was on their immediate agenda. Kirk Hammett had already mentioned that the band had fifteen or so songs ready to move to the next stage, and Hetfield himself had commented on the seemingly relaxed attitude that was prevalent in the studio.

Several things had changed however. Firstly, the writing process was being largely carried out at Metallica HQ, which had become something of a safe haven since the days of *Some Kind Of Monster.*

Secondly, they would have a new producer in the form of Rick Rubin, a guy whose working style was a million miles away from those of Bob Rock or Flemming Rasmussen. Where the latter two preferred a close day-to-day involvement, Rubin's style was deliberately more detached – with fewer visits to the studio to listen to progress.

"Rick Rubin wanted us to focus on the essence of Metallica," Hetfield told MTV. "His essence was around *Master Of Puppets*. He was trying to get us to think, *What were we thinking back then? What were we doing? What were we feeling? What were we influenced by?* Yes, it's interesting homework, but it's impossible to go backwards. We're evolvers, we like moving forward."

Hetfield was absolutely correct of course, it would be pointless to try and recreate a mood whose origins lay twenty years in the past, but the fact that Rubin was making the band *think* while keeping his own creative distance, certainly seemed to be the refreshing tonic Hetfield needed.

While there is no doubt that Rock's brilliant input had worked, it now seemed that the atmosphere in the studio was working pretty well too. Hetfield himself had been heard to comment that Rubin's style now suited him, and that the way he worked from a distance actually took some pressure off.

Therefore, with a favourable environment in place, there was every opportunity for Hetfield and Metallica to come up with their best possible work. Rubin's regime was different in another way too, because in his world Metallica would go nowhere near a recording studio until all the songs in question were as close to complete as possible (in the past the band had often entered the studio with the songs only at demo stage).

Armed with the songs that were being considered for the new album, on March 14 Metallica and their recording crew left HQ for Sound City Studios in Van Nuys, Los Angeles: the venue for the initial part of recording duties. This would be the first time Metallica had recorded outside of the Bay Area since 1991s 'Black' album, and the studio they were using – Sound City – was famous for being the birthplace of Nirvana's seminal slab of grunge immortality called *Nevermind*.

All that was really known at that time was that there was

a possibility of a return to some longer, more complex songs – welcome news for older fans maybe – and that the band aimed to have recording finished by the autumn, in time for an album release date in early 2008.

As time passed however, that prediction would prove highly optimistic. Although new material had been aired – in early form admittedly – at shows in Berlin and later Tokyo, Robert Trujillo revealed that of the two new songs aired, only segments of them would actually end up on the finished album.

During the summer of 2007, Metallica still had several touring commitments, not least an appearance at the Live Earth concert on July 7, followed by a concert at Wembley Stadium the following day. While dedicating themselves fully to the live shows they had on their plate, there was little doubt that the new record was foremost in Metallica's collective minds, even this far from a likely release date.

In the same interview that he had discussed new songs with Greek magazine *Rock Hard,* Trujillo also commented on how the album might end up sounding. "I would say that this album is dynamic, heavy, groovin' and you'll probably be excited to know that there will be guitar solos on it! In addition, Lars remembered to tune his snare drum properly this time!"

In a television interview with NTV, Hetfield explained what the new record represented to him: "It's like opening a new chapter of a book," he explained. "*St. Anger* was a cleansing of all our issues from the past. [The new album] *Death Magnetic* feels new, feels fresh. New bass player, new producer, new attitude in the band, new gratitude in the band. So there is really a new feel."

While Hetfield was a far more amenable interview than possibly any time previously, Trujillo was clearly settling in well to offer such an amusing response to questions about the new Metallica album. The fact that he'd bedded in so impressively on a musical level must have surely helped his confidence. Simply put, Robert Trujillo was exactly the kind of upbeat, humorous guy that Metallica needed, and the fact that he could play brilliantly was a huge bonus also.

Some people saw Trujillo's presence as something even more significant too. "Robert is the best possible guy they could have on board, and it might well be that he is instrumental for making the band function better," says Eric Braverman, who knows Trujillo personally.

As time continued to drag on, it became blatantly obvious that the February release date would not be met, and an official statement stating that the release of the new album entitled *Death Magnetic* would not be until September of that year later confirmed that fact.

Instead of documenting this album's birth retrospectively as they had done with *St. Anger*, Metallica chose to offer the fans a telling insight into their progress via the official Metallica website. Entitled *Mission:Metallica*, small excerpts of footage from the studio appeared as the release date approached. Gradually the fans were given tasters of how the music sounded, and on May 22, the band announced that the recording of *Death Magnetic* was complete. Rick Rubin's job done, all that remained was for engineer Greg Fidelman to mix the album.

Prior to that announcement however, Metallica had been gearing up for the upcoming *Death Magnetic* touring schedule by appearing on that year's Ozzfest line-up. This touring package had been in existence since 1996 and each year the interest in it had been on the increase, to the point that it had become a significant event on the summer schedule. Shadows Fall, originally founded in Springfield, Massachusetts back in 1995, were one of the bands who filled the support slots on Ozzfest 2008. "We were lucky enough to play with them when they headlined," Shadows Fall's singer Brian Fair recalls. "They did a little barbecue afterwards, and they were cool enough to let all the opening bands watch them sound-check. Fair was very clearly impressed with Hetfield's attitude to hospitality, and in many ways, it was unexpected, as he explains: "Some bands pull all that ego shit and clear you away when they are sound-checking. But here's the biggest fuckin' metal band on the planet and they are throwing everyone a barbecue."

In addition to the arena-sized Ozzfest shows, Metallica also ended up doing some more low-key (supposedly) appearances at unlikely locations in the US. One such appearance took place at Pima County Fairgrounds near Tucson, Arizona on May 16. Guess who was there? Yes, you're right, Eric Braverman.

"This thing was almost all the way into Mexico, and they were doing a low-key, or so they thought, show, for a radio station that does not play Metallica [Last.FM]. 30, 000 people showed up out of nowhere in the desert," Braverman enthuses. "Mexicans, Indians. They were climbing fuckin' lampposts to see this show. It was at a fairground so I took a deep fryer so I could fry Twinkies, and candy – just generally to fry shit. Anyway, I put this thing about sixty feet from Lars's drum kit. Everybody all of a sudden starts saying, 'What the hell?' But what was cool was that Peter Mensch really liked my idea and started eating fried Twinkies with me.

That day, James came right up to me and said, 'Hey, Arizona guy, how are you doing?' I was with one of my best friends who had his son with him, and James signed all his stuff, [playfully] hit me on the head and walked off wearing a Cliff Burton tribute t-shirt." Hetfield was friendly that day, and when the show actually started, that amiable side of him continued. "When I watched the show, I sat on the stage with them, and he was making funny faces at me and shit. It was insane."

When it came to actually mixing *Death Magnetic*, Greg Fidelman was ready to roll now that the album was recorded. Fidelman's resume was impressive too, with engineering credits on albums by Johnny Cash, U2, Slipknot and Audioslave, among a vast list of others. Regardless of his experience, the task of mixing a Metallica album represented one of his most high-profile assignments to date, and he simply *had* to get it right – particularly given the *St. Anger* disappointment.

As the excitement built up towards the September release date. Metallica headed to the desert outside Los Angeles to the record the video for the lead single that was to be called 'The Day That Never Comes'. Shortly afterwards, it was announced on the Metallica website that *Death Magnetic* was indeed mixed and mastered, and on September 1, the video for 'The Day That Never Comes' debuted on Metallica.com. Eight days later, Metallica's eighth studio album – comprising ten tracks – was unleashed on the ears of the waiting world.

The cover art that adorned the various *Death Magnetic* 'experiences' (the record was available in several different formats) was what looked like a submerged coffin, and the inspiration for the title was apparently a photograph of the late Alice In Chains singer Layne Staley. Seemingly, Hetfield saw the album as a tribute to what he called rock 'n' roll martyrs, and Staley, being one of them, was the reason for the name of the album.

"... Thinking about death ..." Hetfield told KTV, "some people are drawn towards it – just like a magnet. Other people push [it away]. Also the concept that we're all gonna die sometimes is over-talked about and then a lot of times never talked about – no one wants to bring it up; it's the big white elephant in the living room. But we all have to deal with it at some point." Was this album title the first time a forty-five-year-old James Hetfield had faced the icy grasp of his own mortality? Had his spell of introspection made him think differently about the subject of life and death? Rex Brown suspects that may be the case. "We got close during the time when we were on tour together, we'd text back and forward. James is a very, knowledgeable, down-to-earth person. If you take care of mind, body and soul, everything is okay. After you've been through all the stuff that rock 'n' roll throws at you, there comes a point where you look and say, 'Thank you'."

With a title related to death, it is rather appropriate that the album should begin with a sound synonymous with life. Creeping in with the barely audible sound of a heartbeat, 'That Was Just Your Life' is *Death Magnetic*'s first track. A clean, sinister intro, mildly reminiscent of 'Enter Sandman' leads straight into a satisfyingly powerful guitar salvo of considerable power and authority. Ulrich's drums have a similarly crunchy feel too – worlds away from *St. Anger* – and when the choppy riff dials-in, the Metallica of 2008 really hit the ground running. While certainly not thrash metal as we know it from the 1980s, the sound is significantly more menacing than anything since ... *And Justice For All*, and Hetfield's vocals certainly seem to have recaptured some of his old vitriol.

Track two, 'The End Of The Line', maintains the form too, albeit with more of a groove-based sound akin to some of the *Load*-era material. But as a statement of where Hetfield and his band are in 2008, these beginnings are very promising indeed. 'Broken, Beat And Scarred' is one of the weaker tracks musically, despite being one of Hetfield's more meaningful lyrical outings here, clearly referencing his own durability through personal crisis.

First single 'The Day That Never Comes' follows, and it had already become popular with the fans courtesy of its epic intro and punchy chorus structure. Not a short song by even Metallica's lengthy standards, it loses its way just a touch during the middle with intricate and rather meandering soloing. But at least there *are* solos however, and as a lead single, it was a strong choice on a commercial level.

'All Nightmare Long' is next, and despite being one of James's least favourite songs on the album apparently, it is one of the more complex affairs here, courtesy of some insanely tight Hetfield rhythm work. The riff actually appeared during the *St. Anger* sessions, and while radically altered here, it does illustrate that the material Metallica worked on back then had at least some worth – under the right conditions.

Although it received an advance airing at a few live shows, 'Cyanide' is by far *Death Magnetic's* low point. It is all too predictable sadly, and the strange chorus just does not work at all. 'Unforgiven III' is the weakest in the song's irritating trilogy. String sections and overblown orchestral drama abound, and while perfectly pleasant, it is just not what Metallica do best. The kind of track that suits much better is 'The Judas Kiss' – for many the new album's zenith. A lurching, jagged riff reminiscent of material from *Master Of Puppets*, plus some satisfyingly delivered Hetfield bile really make this track a live favourite, and as a statement of Metallica's self in 2008 it's as good as any.

Instrumental tracks have been a feature of several Metallica albums, particularly in the early years, but sadly 'Suicide And Redemption' does not rival any of the previous greats in terms of drama or complexity. Album closer 'My Apocalypse' is thankfully highly satisfying, and by the far the speediest track on the record. Frenetic Hetfield riffing and some acerbic lyrics make the track the closest thing to what we would call true thrash, and the perfect way to close *Death Magnetic*. Slayer comparisons were mentioned too. While *Death Magnetic* definitely had its failings, there was little doubt that it was a successful exercise and arguably Metallica's best record in twenty years.

Hetfield's rehab period certainly seemed to have helped his creativity, and for many his lyrics and song-writing were back to near top form. The mainstream press were almost all praising of the record, and more than a few suggested that it was a full return to greatness for the band. *Death Magnetic* may not have been a full return to genuine old-school thrash, but for many fans it was at least a significant improvement on everything since 1991. Not just that, Hetfield himself seemed to have rediscovered some of the lyrical bite that had been missing on the mid-1990s output.

As always, not everyone agreed. Malcolm Dome has his own view on the record. "In some ways *Death Magnetic* was the band compromising for the first time in their career. It was almost as if they had said, 'What do people want from us?', rather than them saying, 'This is who we are, this is what we are, this is what we're giving you, make your own mind up'. I don't like the album at all, and I don't think it's really *their* album."

What also came up however was the album's rather unusual sound – hardly a new issue for a Metallica album. Many critics and listeners suggested the sound was suffering from an overly compressed dynamic range in an attempt to increase volume: a problem that resulted in too much distortion. There is little doubt that there is something quite strange about *Death Magnetic's* sound. Q Prime management were keen to bury the matter, and Cliff Burnstein and later Lars Ulrich both came out in public to say that they were happy with the final product.

Most people seemed happy with *Death Magnetic*, and almost all were impressed with Hetfield's contribution to an album that certainly bore his lyrical and musical imprint. *The Guardian* kept it simple when they announced, "[It's] the strongest material the band have written in twenty years." The UK's *Uncut* magazine was similarly pleased with what the band had to offer, saying, "Like all the best heavy rock albums, it suspends your disbelief, demands your attention and connects directly with your inner adolescent." Perhaps a little dramatic, but we know what they meant.

Straight after the release, the band headed into the live arena with important shows in Europe, most notably a Metallica fan-club event at London's 02 Arena on September 15. Three days previously the band had again swung by the *Later With Jools Holland* show, this time performing three songs: 'The Day That Never Comes', 'Cyanide' and 'Enter Sandman' to a rousing reception. There would be no let-up whatsoever, as ahead lay a comprehensive touring schedule involving unforgiving exposure to US audiences beginning in Glendale, Arizona on October 21. David Ellefson went along to the show, and later caught up with James backstage. "I had a great conversation with James. It was really good, we've got families and we've been through some things in our lives. Sometimes we find common ground as gentleman, because our lives are much richer with experience now. I did not notice that when he was on-stage, he was glowing ... he was beaming. I mean, he's been very open about some of the transitions he's been through in his life, and I can relate to some of that myself."

Ellefson himself was raised in a fairly strict Christian background, and after having struggled with some of the usual excesses that the rock world can present, he had himself found the need to come back to a more disciplined, Christian way of thinking. "I'm always happy to see other people succeeding when they go through a transition, and when I saw him I thought, 'He's got it man. He's got the spirit – he's got the fire in him'. He was glowing like a golden angel and I'll never forget it. I was sitting there thinking, 'As big as this is – 20,000 people all wearing Metallica shirts – I really got an impression that there is something even bigger for James than Metallica, or even life after Metallica, kind of in the same way that Bono is. [Bono] has really got into the Holy Spirit and he exudes something far beyond U2, as big as rock music is. I saw that in James too, and my hope for him as a friend is that it continues. A lot of people struggle with these kinds of transitions, and it was nice to see that James was being successful in it."

In addition to Hetfield being in a seemingly happy personal head-space, the band had had sufficient warm-up shows to ensure that the new Metallica live experience was great for all concerned. 'World Magnetic' – as the tour would be called – was perhaps a little unusual, simply because the support acts involved were changed at regular intervals, and that was no bad thing. For example, the first US shows in October and November featured heavy super-group Down and prehistoric doom merchants Sword as guests. December saw metal up-and-comers Lamb Of God stand in, with the exception of the two shows at the LA Forum which had Machine Head on the bill instead. Down was an appropriate choice as support, not least because their bass player was none other than ex-Pantera rumbler Rex Brown. Phil Anselmo was already working on the Down project, when – in one of rock's most shocking events – guitarist Dimebag Darrell was shot dead in 2004 at a show in Columbus, Ohio while on-stage with his new band Damageplan. The shockwaves of such a tragic event reverberated hugely around the rock world, with many acts questioning security issues and worrying about their own safety. "We got the first part of the 'World Magnetic' tour, which was really cool. James and I would talk every night about certain stuff – and it didn't always have to be about recovery. We bonded on a certain level."

Rex and James clearly had similar views on a lot of life's challenges, and he feels strongly about public and media intrusion issues. "Everybody knows that James is sober now, but it's really none of anyone's fuckin' business." Dave Marrs made a point of going along to one of the gigs in southern California. "There were three shows here in southern California, and I actually saw James's sister at one of those shows. We still see her from time to time as a matter of fact." The results of the rotating support were refreshing too, and with different bands on the bill at various stages, 'World Magnetic' had a very exciting feel.

On December 2, 'World Magnetic' swung into Vancouver, with a show at the GM Place. Canada has always been a hot-bed of metal, and Annihilator would rank very highly on any fan's list of vital Canadian thrash outfits. Formed in 1984, Annihilator was actually founded in Ottawa, and their main man was, and still is a supremely gifted guitar player by the name of Jeff Waters. To say that Waters has virtuosic guitar skills would actually be doing the guy a disservice – he's better than that. But as a band, Annihilator just didn't always get the attention they deserved, despite some excellent albums in the 1980s of which 1989's *Alice In Hell* is the high-water mark.

Given that their two bands had relatively similar time-lines, you would have thought that Hetfield and Waters's paths may well have crossed, particularly given their status as two of metal's best axemen. Not so. The two had never met. "I was in Australia mixing a band," Waters explains. "I intentionally stopped over on the way to Vancouver to see the Metallica show. I had heard the new record and thought it had a vibe of the ... *And Justice For All*-era, and it was something I couldn't miss – to see them again."

Waters's means of access was Lamb Of God's Willie Adler, and after the show Waters and he met up. "I said to Willie, 'Any chance I can meet the guys?' And he says, 'Fuck yeah, you don't know them already?' I think I met Kirk first, and he said, 'Jeff! I thought you were from Ottawa?' And I'm looking at Kirk Hammett thinking, 'How the fuck did he know I was from Ottawa?'"

What Jeff was forgetting of course – and it's probably because he's a modest guy – was that although the bands had never actually met, a shrewd student of the guitar game like Hammett was certainly going to be well aware of him and his band. "I didn't see Lars, and then James came in," Jeff continues. "And that was like meeting God. God just walked in the room, and I only ever had that feeling with Robert Plant before, maybe Angus Young. So there I am in a room with James Hetfield, the only guy I have ever got all shaky for, and Willie says, 'Go talk to him!' So I go over and say, 'Hi, my name is Jeff', and I might have said, 'I'm a huge fan of yours' and that was the end of the conversation."

Waters realises now what his mistake was. "I hadn't said my name was Jeff Waters, and that might have been a stupid mistake by me." Waters's chance had gone for now, but he would get a chance to redeem himself later in the tour in Ottawa. Jeff's story illustrates the huge aura that James Hetfield continues to command, and this is even the case for established rock musicians like Jeff. Hetfield is truly an icon, and although his ways of dealing with his fame have necessarily had to change over the years, the effect he has on those around him is undiminished.

Touring business continued through until the end of 2008, before the band were due to head over to Europe for the first part of that leg of the tour. Before they did that, James had the chance to reconnect with yet another face from the early days in Downey, this time Jim Arnold. "Last year I was able to get in touch with him. I had not talked to him since the 'Black' album tour at the LA Forum," Arnold recalls. "He left tickets and backstage passes for me and another old friend [James Ungeheier], so we got to meet with him (almost in private), just James Ungeheier, his daughter, my son and me. He talked to us for about 45 minutes. It was very cool. I am amazed to see that after all his success that he is the same cool guy we use to hang out with back in the day. He doesn't seem to have changed a bit!"

Hindsight had changed a few things for Jim, but the main thing was his thoughts about James's ambitions. "Looking back now," Arnold ponders, "I would say that James was someone who really pursued the 'rock star' dream. He dedicated all of his time to it, and out of all of the musician friends that we knew he seemed to be the most serious. I don't think any of us back then really expected him, or anyone else we knew, to make it big."

With Machine Head and Sword as back-up, Metallica took the arena-sized 'World Magnetic' venues by storm, with a refreshing feature of UK shows being the vastly changing set-lists. While new songs were definitely a welcome feature of the tour in general, something else was different. "I used to be able to predict when James Hetfield would burp on-stage," Eric Braverman reckons. "Now I don't even know what songs they are going to play. It wasn't only that though ..."

For years, James Hetfield had taken pleasure in the gratuitous and humourous use of expletives between numbers. "I remember shows where James would stand there and just see how many swear words he could run together consecutively. Just for the hell of it," Eric Braverman recalls. "Instead of [swearing], now there's beach-balls. The irony is, in the days when he did cuss all the time, Metallica would deliver a cookie-cutter set, playing the same fifteen songs as every other night."

As well as set variation, Braverman was obviously referring to the rather family nature of the modern Metallica show, where James would only use polite and at times motivational terminology when engaging with the fans. While obviously an indication of his own growth since rehab, Hetfield's distinctly polite approach unavoidably changed the feel of a Metallica show.

At the end of every 'World Magnetic' show, a large amount of Metallica logo beach balls were released onto the stage from a net high above, allowing the band to goof around while playing their final encore which was usually 'Seek And Destroy'. All great fun, but hardly the kind of thing you could have imagined James Hetfield doing if you had seen him stripped to the waist and in a Jagermeister-induced haze back in the mid-1980s. But things had changed. That was over twenty years ago.

What this represented was two things. Firstly, rock concerts – and for that matter society as a whole – has undergone a process in recent years, placing much more emphasis on making events family friendly. Secondly, Metallica are a huge corporate beast nowadays, so *everything* is branded, even to the extent of that sea of oversized Metallica beach balls.

What seems to be a likely explanation is that family is much more important in Hetfield's life, therefore that trend has been carried forward into his professional life too. "I saw James at one of the first shows after his rehab and he looked very robotic and very tentative," old friend John Kornarens recalls "As time went on, he's gotten better. I saw them last year and he looked totally confident – he looked great. I was happy for him because I've known him a long time, and now he has kids, I hope he finds some real balance. He has everything he could ever want money-wise. I think he's in a great spot nowadays, and somehow he has survived."

Hetfield certainly had survived, and his obvious confidence and happy demeanour during these early shows of 'World Magnetic' was definitely a very encouraging sign. The tour rolled on through the East Coast and the Mid-West during January, and in February the awards came pouring in for *Death Magnetic* at the Grammy's.

A slew of prestigious awards came their way this time, including 'Best Recording Package' for the album, 'Best Metal Performance' for 'My Apocalypse', 'Best Rock Instrumental' for 'Suicide And Redemption', 'Best Rock Album' for *Death Magnetic*, and finally a 'Best Producer' award for Rick Rubin. Of perhaps more significance was the announcement that Metallica were to be inducted into the Rock 'n' Roll Hall Of Fame in 2009, with a ceremony scheduled for April 4, in Cleveland, Ohio. While that was obviously a hugely important announcement, and one that was certainly overdue, when the day came around, it would also take on a new meaning in the life and career of James Hetfield.

Before any of this happened, the band had some important European dates to fulfil, including two stunning shows at the O2 Arena in London at either end of March. Both concerts were stunning in their own right, and worlds apart from the rather more scrappy fan club gig the previous year.

However, the most significant feature was the vastly different set lists that were used, both of which drew material from the band's *entire* back-catalogue. Obviously, the *Death Magnetic* material got a consistently thorough airing – with some weaker album moments like 'Cyanide' translating really well to the live arena. It was the unexpected introduction of tracks like 'Fight Fire With Fire' and 'Outlaw Torn' that really provided interesting variation though, to the point that the Metallica live experience had now become *compelling* rather than predictable. The tour broke for much of the month of April, and the band prepared for what was sure to be an emotional day in Cleveland on the fourth, with several ghosts of the past ripe for exorcism.

Chapter 16

Friends Again?

Scheduled for official induction on that incredible day in Cleveland were the existing band members, along with two bass players Jason Newsted and the late Cliff Burton. In addition to that, Hetfield made the decision to invite pretty much everyone who had been involved with the history of Metallica. Apart from being a considerable financial gesture (everyone was flown-in at the band's expense, and accommodated in top hotels), it was also an unprecedented move of friendship. "I saw James at the Rock 'n' Roll Hall Of Fame and it was a great trip. They flew us all in for the show," Lloyd Grant recalls. "He invited me to Cleveland, and that was very cool," Ron McGovney enthuses. "I hadn't hooked up with James for a few years and I noticed a difference. The most significant thing about him was that he is very confident about himself now. He was very shy all those years ago. He absolutely grabs the attention of everyone who is in the same room with him now. Not just that, he later invited me and my kids to the shows at Charlotte and Atlanta, and James went out of his way to make my kid's first concert experience, one that they will never, ever forget."

While McGovney would not be officially inducted (he had never actually played on an album), it did seem that his invitation to attend was meant as a belated, but generous acknowledgement of all his work and dedication to Metallica in those formative days. The Cleveland trip was a joyous gathering of many people from Metallica's past, and the mood was one of mutual appreciation, respect and gratitude on all fronts. "The band performed the unprecedented act of flying people in from all over the world – close to 200 – who were part of their journey from the Bay Area garages to global domination. James was sober and friendly, shaking hands and exchanging words with every guest who attended. Me included," Lonn Friend remembers.

The ceremony itself was an emotional affair. With faltering acceptance speeches from all inducted, and an up-beat speech from the late Cliff Burton's father Ray, it really was a choker to see the band on-stage to join legends of the rock world. It was appropriate also that at a ceremony involving no less than three bass players, the induction itself should be performed by another member of the four-string alliance – Flea from the Red Hot Chilli Peppers.

Jason Newsted's presence was particularly special, and his speech was warmly emotional too – concluding with that timeless acknowledgement to Metallica's millions of worldwide fans: "Without you, there could be no us" – hitting home particularly powerfully while Newsted himself visibly fought back tears.

Hetfield himself was calm and very assured behind the microphone too. Exuding an almost amazing level of positivity, James was a revelation that evening, and as David Ellefson had alluded to previously, he really looked and behaved as if he was operating on an almost ethereal level. "I'd like to give some huge gratitude to my higher power. For the gift of music and the awareness of my destiny early on," Hetfield said. "Music is my therapy, and I need to do it. I would love to thank my wife Francesca for saving my life ... many times. My children, all three of you are here. Thank you for teaching me how to love ..."

Despite the highly charged emotional content, Hetfield's demeanour that evening in Cleveland was without doubt the culmination of a lifetime of hurt, hard work and incredible success. "This is living proof," Hetfield roared while pounding the podium, "that it is possible to make a dream come true."

Hetfield finished by thanking Lars Ulrich for 'calling him' all those years ago, and by doing so, including him in his dream to become part of the biggest heavy metal band in the world. With that, he turned and picked up the diminutive and grinning Ulrich in a bear hug that you just knew was genuine, and brought the audience in attendance to its feet.

Almost an irrelevance on that evening was the actual musical performance. Taking to the stage again with his old friends, Newsted roared through renditions of 'Enter Sandman' and

'Master Of Puppets', followed by an encore version of Aerosmith's 'Train Kept-A-Rollin' alongside Johnny Burnette & The Rock 'n' Roll Trio.

The Cleveland weekend was a momentous occasion for all concerned, and it definitely seemed to be a turning point in that James seemed happy to re-connect with key people from his past. What followed in future months was a continuing commitment to reconnect with former friends and associates. As the 'World Magnetic' extravaganza rolled on, several old faces were welcomed back. One such face was that of Michael Alago, with whom James had lost contact for many years. Alago himself confirms that it was great to re-connect with James when the band played in New York at Madison Square Garden. "I haven't really kept in touch with James but I saw him backstage and thought he looked awesome ... all grown up of course, and now he seemed like a very focused man and performer." There was certainly a general move going on during 'World Magnetic' to embrace many of the personalities from the past who had for one reason or another become distant to Metallica's ascent into mega-stardom.

After all the excitement of Cleveland, the band had to regroup and take 'World Magnetic' back on the road to Europe. This was to be an intense period of touring activity too, and yet while the campaign was generally waged in Europe, Metallica still managed three consecutive shows in Mexico City during early June.

July was unforgiving also, and before returning to US soil, the band took part in the Sonisphere series of festival shows, a trek that culminated in a triumphant homecoming on August 2 at Knebworth House, England, the scene of Led Zeppelin's two mammoth gigs back in 1979.

While that Knebworth performance was by no means their best of that summer, (Hetfield and Hammett's guitar parts were unusually sloppy), it did signal the end, for the time being at least, of a gripping assault on the European mainland. Not just that, Metallica's set ended in the early hours of August 3, James Hetfield's forty-sixth birthday.

Touring continued to grind out the autumn months, much of that time through the East coast, Mid-West and Canada. When the tour came to Ottawa, Jeff Waters got an opportunity to redeem himself. "I talked to James about Michael Alago, but I didn't really get a chance to have much of a longer conversation with him."

As to James's demeanour after that Ottawa show, Waters was pensive: "Kirk Hammett was almost hugging me, that's how warm and friendly he seemed. James seemed to be ten feet taller than he really is, and just very guarded." Jeff expands on his observation: "I'm making that assessment based on years of reading people. He's very much as if he has a wall up … when the wall comes down, they're normal guys and nice guys, But when you're as famous as James is, you have to have that wall there to protect yourself."

Waters' observation is correct, and the reason for it is simple, as he explains: "When you get to know people like James, I'm sure they are super-nice guys. But can you imagine the tens of millions of people who want to get to know that guy? It's a fuckin' corporation they are running, and they just can't let everyone in."

With the 'World Magnetic' tour pausing for much needed breath on December 12, Metallica received another Grammy Nomination for the following year's ceremony, when 'Unforgiven III' was earmarked by the panel in the 'Best Hard Rock Performance' category. With their year at an end, it was time to reflect on a colossally effective restoration of their position in the larger metal tapestry.

While other acts appeared on the scene and threatened to take things to a much higher level (Mastodon being a good example), no band on Earth could live with Metallica's crushing economic might. Forget that *Death Magnetic* is a fairly 'safe' record by Metallica's standards. The fact of the matter is that with staggering sales figures, and an ascent to Number 1 in no fewer than thirty-four countries, *Death Magnetic*'s job was already done. The bottom line is that Metallica are back as the biggest band on planet Earth, and that situation doesn't look like changing so long as the will to be there remains.

The last word on that is best left to Down's Rex Brown, who from his position in the audience each night on the tour made the following observation: "I stood in the same exact spot every night. Every time during 'For Whom The Bell Tolls', James would come up and hit my hand," Rex continues. "And all I am thinking is, '*This* is the band I met twenty five years ago. They've sold over

100 million records and I can't believe it ... that they've come full-circle like this."

Chapter 17

Guitar Hero

Some Kind Of Monster, while undoubtedly a painful exercise for James Hetfield, was without doubt the best way that information could have been made available to the public domain. Without its stark honesty about Hetfield, all we would have had access to would have been speculation and rumour and those, in most cases, are worse than the truth itself.

As human beings, we all encounter problems in life, and although Hetfield's were a matter of public interest because of who he is, they are in fact no different from those of millions of human beings all around the world. As this author stated at the very start of this book, the environment a person grows up in can significantly influence every aspect of their later life, and given that James Hetfield had a notably tougher start to life than most, it is a miracle that he has become the man he has. As he said himself, music has been his therapy, and that is the bottom line.

To fully appreciate exactly what it is that makes James's musical abilities so vital to rock music, we should probably concentrate on the opinions and testimony of his many peers, simply because they know what it takes to actually hit such stellar heights. Alex Skolnick, a hugely talented musician both within the parameters of heavy metal as well as something of a virtuoso in other styles of music too, definitely believes that James has a very special talent. "I'm convinced that had he chosen to play drums, bass or lead guitar in his band, James would have been just as influential and virtuosic." Skolnick definitely has a point, especially when you consider that at various points in his career, James successfully fulfilled all of the above roles.

Hugh Tanner certainly agrees with Skolnick's suggestion, and having been physically present during those formative years in

Brea, he is surely better qualified than most to comment. "James could sit at the piano and sound good and he could sit behind a drum kit and play. In fact, at that time ... he would have been a better drummer than Lars."

Hetfield's destiny however was with the guitar, and it is there that the true depth of the man's musical ability really lies. Whether it is his clinically tight rhythm delivery, or his contrastingly loose and soulful lead work, Hetfield has it all, as Alex Skolnick suggests: "As a rhythm guitarist, he has had more of an impact on the guitar than most lead guitarists. A great lead guitarist himself, [his] occasional solos are among Metallica's most memorable, proving that speed and chops are secondary to melody." In a guitar world where skill and worth are increasingly judged on outlandish technical wizardry, Skolnick's assessment of the solidity of Hetfield's playing is even more apt.

It does not end there for Alex either: "He is also a fine acoustic guitarist, playing intricate parts with a lot of depth, consistency and dynamics." That much is also true, and while much of that acoustic skill is probably borne out of endless hours on a tour bus, with little access to amplified sound, it is also possible that his interest in country, blues and folk styles have made this side of his guitar playing that much more polished.

Mille Petrozza, for many people the king of true European thrash (and like James, a singer and rhythm guitarist himself), shares Skolnick's opinion: "To be honest, I have lost track of them since the 'Black' album. I still respect them for everything they've done, but for some reason I could never get into the country/rock/alternative touch they put into their music since the 1990s. But despite feeling that way about the music, I still think that he is one of the best, if not *the* best rhythm guitarist in all of metal."

Lonn Friend is one of the few non-band members to witness the riff-lord himself in the studio, having been present on a daily basis at the 'Black' album sessions. "In modern hard rock history, no one stands any taller than James Hetfield. He defined the speed metal rhythm riff and transitioned what was once fodder for the underground into mainstream success."

So what is it exactly about Hetfield's guitar technique that makes him stand like a bare-chested colossus above all the other metal wannabees? Joel McIver's book *The 100 Greatest Metal Guitarists* is a comprehensive assessment of all the great players within the genre, and his section about James gives excellent insight into his significance. "Hetfield scraped away at the strings like some kind of single-minded robot, cupping his hand around the bridge for a perfectly taut sound that made heavy metal sound not brash nor rude nor sexy but more like the future. The apocalypse had arrived, and it came in the shape of the right hand of a spotty teenager from the wrong side of the LA tracks."

McIver captures perfectly the Hetfield guitar persona; Hetfield himself told McIver how he approaches rhythm tempos: "I'm pretty comfortable with my down-picking. I don't see how it could get much faster. It's not a race. It's not really about ability: it's writing a good riff and knowing what tempo it needs to be, where it lives in the song."

The 'down-picking' that Hetfield refers to is a mildly technical guitar term, and for those not familiar with one end of a guitar from another, it's the downward stroke of the plectrum or 'pick' against the strings. Sometimes that down-stroke is followed by an 'up-stroke' in the opposite direction, but in the case of some of Metallica's most effective riffs, the taut sound is as a result of repeated down-strokes only.

Continuing on a technical level, it's worth mentioning that Hetfield's actual physical 'look' while wielding a guitar is a huge contributing factor to his iconic status. While some guitarists look as if the instrument is a six-stringed alien appendage, Hetfield's always looks as if it's a permanent extension of his torso.

While his customary posture – left leg a full step in front of the right, knees slightly bent and back hunched menacingly over the microphone – was undoubtedly more effective in his days of long unruly hair but even now he still cuts a hugely iconic figure, one that you too can try to emulate in your living room, if you so wish.

The guitar itself is part of the look of course, and over the years, Hetfield has brandished a few weapons that we can easily identify with. There is the white ESP Explorer with 'EET FUK' emblazoned on it, although fans won't see this much as it now lies retired in the Rock 'n' Roll Hall Of Fame Museum in Cleveland, Ohio. That guitar suited him perfectly however, and while numerous variations of that off-set Explorer shape have been deployed in battle over the years, nothing looked quite as cool as this one did during the *Master Of Puppets* era.

Of secondary consideration would be his 'Truckster'; another ESP guitar, but this time in the more conservative shape of a Les Paul, which the manufacturer Gibson made famous as far back as the early 1950s. If you revisit the *Some Kind Of Monster* DVD, you'll see Hetfield scratching-out most of *St. Anger's* sludgy riffs on a guitar much like this one.

Of equal significance is James's unusual vocal delivery, which in all truth is not even questioned nowadays because we have become so accustomed to how he sounds. His vocals are not what classicists would call conventional 'singing' in its purest sense – particularly pre-1991 – but there is no doubt that his style during the *Kill 'Em All* and *Ride The Lightning* eras perfectly suited what was a completely new kind of music.

"What I got out of them in the early days was that he wasn't a rock singer," suggests Anthrax's Charlie Benante, who's seen James's progression as a singer from the beginning. "It was all about aggression and angst. You wouldn't consider James a Freddie Mercury type, but it totally paved the way for what was to come."

Chuck Billy does not have the added distraction of playing a guitar while fronting Testament, although he makes up for that by replicating every note of every riff while clutching his microphone stand as if he wished he actually did have a guitar. Chuck is another peer who has a huge amount of respect for James's vocal presence. "To me he was probably one of the first power metal singers, or thrash metal guys that actually came out and had hooks and melodies in the vocals. That's what I really liked about James. How catchy the choruses were and how clever the lyrics were. When you put the music that he was playing on top of all that, I was like 'Wow!' I always thought James was one of the best song-writers and lyricists to date."

Lonn Friend, a man who definitely has a way with words, takes it all one step further: "As a frontman, he delivers each and every night, the growl and groove that has made Metallica what they are. They reign supreme as one of the finest live bands in the history of rock 'n' roll because they leave nothing in the bag. It's a concert bonfire and James holds the brightest torch."

With such glowing testimony from metal peers, you could certainly say that Hetfield has worked hard on his vocal style over the years. When you also consider that for a long time he didn't actually want to be a singer at all, the level he has achieved is a great credit to his perseverance.

There is one more person to thank for that however, and that man is producer Bob Rock. Before the 'Black' album shook Planet Rock to its foundations in 1991, you would have been hard pressed to find many harmonies on previous Hetfield songs. Sure, the band had dabbled in textured vocals on tunes like 'Fade To Black' but there was a feeling that it was half-hearted, and that it wasn't being done with any real confidence.

When Rock arrived on the scene, much of that changed. Because of his background, which involved working with bands whose sound actually relied on harmony, Rock knew that if he could combine Metallica's undoubted muscle with a little vocal finesse, he had a match made in rock heaven.

When Hetfield emerged blinking from the exhaustive process of recording, the results as we all know now were absolutely stunning. While it's accepted that tracks like 'Nothing Else Matters' and 'The Unforgiven' are far removed from the ethos of a thrash metal band, nobody could argue that it was those kinds of harmonies that took Metallica to a completely new level of commercial acceptance. Remember his Brea Olinda High School prediction? *Play music, get rich* ...

No assessment of Hetfield's worth would be complete without an acknowledgement of another part of his incredible armoury. We know he's a great guitarist, we recognise that he's an iconic singer and frontman. We might even be persuaded that James is a very likeable and often misunderstood person. However to justify our imminent placement of James Hetfield among the true legends of popular music, and by that we mean the Dylans, the Springsteens, the U2s and the (brace yourself) the Madonnas, we have to consider his song-writing and lyrical ability.

Forget that Metallica have and still do operate in a genre far removed from all of the above. Song-writing is song-writing. The real test is whether you can sustain it over time, and in a way that propels your band from point A to point B, when others are falling by the wayside. When Metallica came slicing out of the underground, they did so on the back of not just tight riffs, aggressive singing and a 'fuck you' attitude. They did it because of a killer series of songs that seized the attention of an entire generation, and dragged them screaming into the future.

Heavy metal, whether the establishment likes it or not, is a massively influential movement, and when a band comes along that can not only re-invent a genre, but also launch it head-long into the mainstream, their importance simply cannot be ignored.

While Lars Ulrich can take some credit for some of this frightening progress, there is little doubt that his main strengths lie elsewhere. Consequently, in this author's opinion, James Hetfield is the man responsible for much of the song-writing genius that is Metallica, (although obviously Lars and Kirk deserve huge credit also).

When we try to figure out just how a guy like Hetfield has managed to construct such incredible songs, we need only refer to the testimony of that guy from his childhood, Hugh Tanner. All those years ago in a bedroom in Brea, Hugh Tanner knew that the person he was jamming with had a knack of assembling kick-ass rock songs, and all that from just a collection of crudely assembled guitar riffs. Bands like Led Zeppelin managed the same thing of course, but they used a blues-based blueprint that surely made their task that much easier. Hetfield did not have a blueprint as such, but what he did have was a collection of wildly disparate influences, from Aerosmith to The Tygers Of Pan Tang, and the results he came up with sounded like nothing we had ever heard before.

While true fans of Metallica will always have a soft spot for the first four incredible albums, the biggest stroke of genius came in the form of 1991's *Metallica*, where Hetfield, as Lonn Friend said, "used his musical genius to create the monster that is 'Black'."

It's the kind of album that comes along only once or twice every half a century, and that fact alone, combined with its thermonuclear sales success, is sufficient to ensure Hetfield's song-writing immortality. Part of the appeal of these incredible tracks are the lyrics, and Hetfield himself scratches them out in that now familiar spidery style with a painstaking attention to detail, which simply seizes the listener's attention.

Not just that, his lyrics always have a point. They either paint a picture, describe a person, or champion a cause. They are always compelling and sometimes bitter but at the same time witty and sarcastic. Hetfield the master song-writer is also a lyrical genius, and every bit as worthy as a Dylan or a Springsteen in both respects.

But what of James Hetfield? Where does his role fit into the now-evolved Metallica picture? In many ways, he fits in where he always did ... in control.

"James's [has] been in control all the time," Rex Brown suggests. "Lars is the spokesperson, but what James says kinda fuckin' goes, you've seen the movie [*Some Kind Of Monster*], man. Those guys could have got up and left and said, 'Well, fuck you!', you know." Rex believes things are different now, "It's easy to get caught up in thinking that you are some kind of god. James isn't like that and he's brought some of that into the team of Metallica. He realises that he can't always do it all on his own."

Hetfield chooses to conduct himself differently post-rehab, and the way that he now gives insightful, positive interviews as well as tempering the on-stage obscenities would suggest that he's very much mastered himself. Rex Brown feels that James has two sides to him nowadays too. "There is one side to James where he walks into a room and you just shut up," Brown says without a hint of humour. "Then there's another where you can sit down with him and have an honest conversation. He's very intellectual."

"I have always considered James Hetfield to be the consummate professional," says Eric Braverman. "I just can't believe how actually awesome and incredible he can be. Just his guitar playing and singing at the same time, and his lyrics that he writes, Just his whole image is awesome ..." Even though Eric and James have had times where they don't necessarily see eye-to-eye, Braverman still says, "Be in no doubt, his shit is Disney-esque!"

While James's personal battles have thrown a few obstacles in his path over the years, his place in the overall fabric of music is even more important than ever. Malcolm Dome, a man who has observed Hetfield's phenomenal rise to prominence from a critical standpoint over the last twenty-five years, agrees: "I think James is a vitally important figure in music, and I think that importance has become more over the last ten or so years."

The last ten years, while without doubt the most public of Hetfield's incredible career, have also coincided with a radical change in the way that the media and the world in general views people, particularly famous people. Katon de Pena, another old friend of James's from the early days in LA, still keeps in touch via mutual friends like Brian Slagel, and he feels strongly about the personal side of the matter. "James is a great guy. Sometimes I feel that he is misunderstood. I think some people should keep in mind that if you don't really know him ... you don't have the right to judge him."

When rock 'n' roll judgement day arrives, as it surely one day will, James Hetfield's career will be remembered because of his indelible imprint on the history of rock music, not his public personal battles. With that in mind, we will leave the personal side of Hetfield's life where it belongs, and in the safe knowledge that when closely examined, his ascent out of a difficult childhood in Downey should be viewed as nothing other than a fabulous, inspirational success story.

Sadly, thousands of kids just like James Hetfield do not make it, and instead find themselves in frustratingly unfilled situations in life, with no obvious escape route. Instead of having Joe Perry posters on their bedroom wall, they may well have a life-size image of James Hetfield. As Hugh Tanner said, James's story should be an inspiration to any kid out there playing guitar riffs in his bedroom, with the unfaltering dream of becoming a rock star.

James Hetfield's place in popular music is indeed already assured. Forget the staggering record sales, the vast tours, the movies and the accompanying dramas. The bottom line is that he represents what we all want to be, but never dare admit it.

The fact that Metallica recently endorsed their own edition of the insanely addictive *Guitar Hero* series of video games will only perpetuate that feeling. For those of us that cannot play a guitar, strip to the waist and hunch over the microphone like some kind of spitting, snarling caveman, our chance is here. The fact that we would even consider doing that (and millions apparently do), should tell you all you need to know about Hetfield's place in all of this. He's a musical genius and, a living legend. He's also an international treasure.

References

While the bulk of the interviews in this book were conducted by the author on a first-hand basis, there were other sources used – or at least referenced – in order to add important accuracy, colour and depth to the material. They are as follows:

Magazine and Book Sources:
Small interview segments by the author Joel McIver, *Playboy, Thrasher, Music and Sound Output, Metal Hammer, Kerrang!, Billboard, Shockwaves, Rolling Stone, Metal Edge, Guitar World, Guitar, Metallica: The Stories Behind The Biggest Songs, So What* fanzine, *Revolver*.

Online press sources: www.Metallica.com and www.Metworld.co.uk

Television, DVD, Online, Radio and TV Sources:
Some Kind Of Monster official DVD
Classic Albums Series - Metallica
VH1 Behind The Music - Megadeth
Metallica – S&M Official DVD
KTV
NTV
Aardschok

I also include here some other interesting websites connected to some of the contributors to this book. Please check them all out.

www.impbooks.com
www.adrenalinepr.com
www.testamentlegions.com
www.hardradio.com
www.metalblade.com
www.kreator-terrorzone.de
www.annihilatormetal.com
www.down-nola.com
www.pantera.com
www.killingtimeproductions.com
www.sweetsilence.com
www.michaelwagener.com
www.blackdevilrecords.com
www.joelmciver.co.uk
www.thequietus.com
www.davidellefson.com
www.alexskolnick.com
www.totalrock.com
www.aliceinchains.com
www.shadowsfall.com
www.anthrax.com
www.beehlermetal.com
www.theclassicmetalshow.com

Visit our website at *www.impbooks.com*
for more information on our full list
of titles including books on:

Robert Plant, Bruce Dickinson, Rage Against The Machine,
System Of A Down, MC5, Slash, 'Skins', 'Scooter Boys',
Dave Grohl, Muse, Green Day, Ian Hunter,
Mick Ronson, David Bowie, The Prodigy
and many more.